Turn Compassion to ACTION

Real-Life Stories, Practical Tools,
Motivational Guide for Compassion Ministries

Denise Wendle

TURN COMPASSION TO ACTION

Real Life Stories, Practical Tools, Motivational Guide for Compassion Ministries

© 2018 Denise Wendle

ISBN (print version): 978-1-7321721-0-4

ISBN (kindle version): 978-7321721-1-1

Library of Congress Control Number (LCCN): 2018903669

The book has been prepared for publication by Wendy K. Walters and Palm Tree Productions—www.palmtreeproductions.com.

Printed in the United States of America.

To contact the author:
denise.wendle@gmail.com
www.turncompassiontoaction.com

This Book is Dedicated To ...

First and foremost,

My Jesus

My Lord and Savior, My Faithful Friend

My family

My husband, Jeff, and our two sons and their families

Jason and Krista and their three children
Jonah Gabriel, Ezra Andrew, and Anastasia Hope

Ethan and Kristen and their three children
Everley Noelle, Anthem Dei, and Archer Rae

Any additional grandchildren that may arrive
to the Wendle family, whether biological or adopted

May we always turn our compassion to action!

Endorsements

Most people I meet want their lives to make an impact for God, but so many struggle to figure out what their calling is or how to get there. If that resonates with you, I highly recommend *Turn Compassion to Action: How Ordinary People Can Make a Difference* by Denise Wendle. Rolland and I moved to Indonesia with $30 in our pockets with no set plans, and God backed us up. You can also love God and love people right where you are. Denise gives fabulous advice for anyone who does not know what do to: just do something! If you feel passionate for children, start volunteering at youth groups. If you feel passionate to end sex trafficking, find an organization working in that area. One of my life messages is to stop for one person every day who God puts in front of you. In this way, everyone can share God's love and make an impact. Throughout this book, Denise gives spiritual and practical wisdom from her personal experiences of twenty years working in the inner city as well as the experiences of others in ministry. She also provides worship songs, reflection points, and journaling questions to help you apply what you read to your own walk with God. Get this book and allow God to lead you on new adventures one step at a time!

Heidi Baker, PhD
Co-Founder & CEO - Iris Global

This is not a book based upon theories, but written by one who has spent years running a non-profit that did what the book is about. I have known Denise for many years and know that she is passionate about helping the marginalized, and that passion comes through in her book. Having seen thirteen years of graduates from our supernatural ministry training school, and how sometimes, those who graduate know how to pray for the sick and demonized, how to prophesy, and minister by the Spirit; don't know how to run a ministry that ministers to the marginalized on a more wholistic level. This book is an important "how to" book to help those who want to develop and run a sustained ministry to the poor and needy, broken and marginalized. I encourage anyone who is interested in this type of ministry to purchase, read, and refer back to *Turn Compassion to Action: How Ordinary People Can Make a Difference*. It is full of practical advice and instruction.

Randy Clark
Founder - Global Awakening and Global School of Supernatural Ministry
D. Min. Overseer of the Apostolic Network of Global Awakening
Randy Clark's books are available on amazon.com

I first met Denise when she ran the Center for Champions, a wonderful ministry that she founded and dedicated to inner-city children in Harrisburg, PA. Her new book, *Turn Compassion to Action: How Ordinary People Can Make a Difference* is an exciting reminder of God's desire to partner with His children to lift up the poor and needy (Psalm 113). If you have been called to step into a hands-on consistent ministry, then this book is a must-read. More than a "how to" book, Denise points to the sustaining grace of the Cross. You will be freshly inspired by faith-building scriptural insights and the practical wisdom that she has learned along the way.

Georgian Banov
President and Co-Founder - Global Celebration and
Global Celebration School of Supernatural Ministry (GCSSM)

Jesus looks at the teeming masses of humanity and His heart breaks with compassion. He asks us to be his hands and feet in touching their needs. Will we respond? Here is a book that not only challenges us with this imperative, but also how to live lives of bold compassion like our Lord. If you're wanting to live a life that counts, I recommend reading it!

Seth Barnes
Founder - Adventures in Mission
Author - "Kingdom Journeys: Rediscovering the Lost Spiritual Discipline"

For those who desire to do Christian, ministry-oriented social work, this is an excellent resource for helping to develop the spiritual strength to serve others. Denise writes from the heart in providing practical guidance and wisdom on helping to meet the spiritual and practical needs of populations at risk in an urban setting. She craftily weaves real-life stories and personal examples of the successes and challenges of ministry into the pages of this ministry workbook. Denise provides practical tools and genuine advice and encouragement in helping ordinary people make a difference in the lives of the hurting. This excellent Biblically-based resource could be a supplemental reading or classroom workbook to teach social work students how to integrate social work and compassion ministries.

Dr. Charles Seitz
Department Chair and Professor of Social Work - Messiah College

This book, *Turn Compassion into Action*, reminds those of us who work or train others to work in areas of service that you do not have to be called into the 5-fold ministry to make a difference. You can start from where you are. That is what I watched Denise do year in and year out and consequently, the trajectory of individual lives and entire family lines were forever changed for the better. I recommend obtaining this book as a training tool for yourself and for your students. You do not have to be in ministry to use this book as it is for everyone who has ever wondered, "What is going on in the world and what can I do about it?" Take a look inside and it will change the way you look at your job. It may just inspire you to not only find how ordinary people can make a difference but compel you to actually make a difference.

Turn Compassion into Action How Ordinary People Can Make a Difference is an example of a lifetime of devoted service to others!

Dr. Angela Campbell
Professor of Counseling
HACC Central Pennsylvania's Community College

Denise is the real deal! She left her comfort zone and went into the inner-city war zones to fight the destructive forces of hopelessness and poverty. Her profound compassion took her into the deep, establishing an inner-city ministry that continues to change the lives of many. God's love compelled her. Faith was translated into action. The stories in this book are true and moving. Reading this book, you will be motivated to turn your own passion into reality and given practical advice on how to do it. The best life is one that's given away to set others free!

Charles Stock

Senior Pastor - Life Center Ministries
Denise's Pastor!

Denise Wendle has written a loving and challenging book. Loving because it is not preachy or patronizing, but full of empathy and humanity. Challenging because it asks us to face up to our excuses and fears and lack of the kind of responsible commitment that leads to action.

Denise speaks from many years of experience as a wife, mother, counselor and pioneer and comes across with authenticity. I recommend this book for those who are committed to living a Biblical lifestyle and are prepared to actually do something rather than talking about doing something.

Andrew Shearman

Founder - G 42 Leadership Academy
Pastor and Inspirational Speaker

Acknowledgements

I would like to express my sincere gratitude and appreciation to some very special people who have played a significant part in this book coming to completion. I'm grateful for their encouragement, assistance in editing, and great advice. I'm excited about the finished product. I believe that hurting people are going to receive help from those who read this book and take the message to heart. Thanks go out to the following people:

- **Jeff Wendle,** my incredibly supportive husband, who read the first drafts and offered wisdom and some editing advice. He was fonder of commas than my final editor. We gave precedence to the professional.

- **Byron Louw,** a professor and young millennial, who read and liked several of my first attempts at writing, offered advice, and gave much needed positive encouragement to keep going.

- **Amber Good,** a comrade from Center for Champions and a young mother of four, who helped me get serious about writing this book. She offered editing assistance and showed me how much I really use the word "really" and other very helpful grammatical tidbits.

- **Suzie D'Souza,** a young, experienced professional editor who provided invaluable editing assistance. I appreciated her expertise, comments and direction, helping me present a book that others will enjoy reading and hopefully be moved to take action.

- **Wendy K. Walters,** whose motivational Release the Writer class, creative cover design, and publishing company's efforts in formatting, printing, and other assistance brought this book from a dream to a reality.

I would also like to acknowledge several ministry leaders and ministries whose teaching and life examples have had a tremendous effect on my life and on so many others. Their lessons and words are weaved through out this book.

- **Charles and Anne Stock,** senior pastors, and the church body of Life Center Ministries, International. www.lcmi.org

- **Heidi and Rolland Baker,** founders of Iris Global. www.irisglobal.org

- **Randy Clark,** founder of Global Awakening. www.globalawakening.com

- **Georgian and Winnie Banov,** founders of Global Celebration. www.globalcelebration.com

- **Center for Champions,** a mentoring ministry helping inner-city children and families in Harrisburg, Pa. www.centerforchampions.org

Finally, I would like to acknowledge and thank my comrades in ministry who worked many years alongside me at Center for Champions or made a way for it to continue, once I passed the baton. Without these people, Center for Champions would never have been able to continue to help inner-city children and families year after year. I could never have continued that ministry without their help. Thank you, my friends.

- **Linda Semke**
- **Jeff Bruce**
- **Eric and Tara Brenize**
- **Shannon Shelly**
- **Richie Lewis**

Section V—Renewing Your Strength & Preventing Burnout

Section VI—Crossing the Finish Line

Getting the Most Out of This Book

Song Titles that Begin the Chapters

Worship music can encourage those serving in a compassion ministry in so many ways. It can lift us up and usher us into the presence of God. It can remind us of God's faithfulness in the midst of a trying situation. I know it did that for me countless times. Each chapter begins with a title of a worship song that is relevant to the chapter's topic. Listen and make a playlist of these songs, or if you love hymns or another artist, make your own playlist. The key is to find songs that inspire and encourage you as you minister to the hurting.

Reflection and Action Sections

For those who wish to study the chapter topics further, notice the devotional section at the end of each chapter. There's the featured song under *Listen*. Under *Study*, Bible verses or readings are listed. Under *Journal*, questions are asked that will hopefully encourage you to engage in thoughtful self-examination and inspire you to think about the topics discussed in more depth.

Recommended Resources

Located at the back of the book, there is an extensive list of resources on different topics that have proven helpful in ministry. These are ones that have impacted myself and numerous other believers. Much of this list comes from my opportunity over the past twenty years of being a part of Life Center Ministries, as I attended numerous conferences and classes that were offered.

Many of these books, and other media, along with some of the online courses have been incredibly useful to people serving in compassion ministry. In addition, there are references to various online trainings that are available to help those who want to grow in knowledge and skills as they provide inner healing and prayer counseling.

Appendix

Suggestions for the kinds of forms and useful material one might need in an incorporated compassion ministry, especially if a ministry involves working with children, are provided in this section at the end of the book.

Reading - Turn Compassion to Action

This book can be read in the traditional manner—from cover to cover. However, I have designed many of the chapters to stand alone, so that they can be easily referred to when an issue arises that fits the topic of a specific chapter. My heart is that this book would encourage and inspire you to step out in faith and also be a practical resource to help you do so.

Running the Race Helping the Hurting

God Uses Ordinary People

Writing a book was not something I thought I would ever do. Nor did I ever imagine that I would co-found and lead an inner-city ministry for sixteen years. Yet God calls you and me to run races that are unexpected, and that are simultaneously difficult and rewarding.

This book is for those who have never walked on water, and probably never will. Not that I believe it's impossible. It's just that we associate the bold and courageous ones with such acts and this book is geared to the less than brave, the ordinary ones. The ones who may hesitate to put their toes in the water. The good news is that God delights in using ordinary people. After all, Jesus' disciples included fishermen, a tax collector, and even a guy known as "doubting" Thomas. And these humble men were used by God in the first century to reach the world with the gospel. Even Peter, the only one of the twelve who did, in fact, walk on water, denied Jesus *three* times because he was afraid. I've been amazed and grateful to have known a few modern-day giants in the faith who have seen thousands come to Christ, and seen thousands more miraculously healed through their ministries. But you don't have to be a giant in the faith to be used by God or to make a difference in someone's life.

God is calling you and me—the everyday people with tender hearts that bleed when we hear about the pain, the hurting, the injustice, and

1

the needs of others. Your tender heart is just the spark that God can use to light a fire of redemptive love that will change somebody's world.

Why Write a Book?

I first started feeling God nudge me toward developing this book several years ago when I was taking a break from leading Center for Champions, the after-school ministry that I started in Harrisburg, Pennsylvania in 1998. Discouraged and battling Lyme disease, I was reflecting on how the ministry had not reached as many families as I had hoped. But as I realized how much I had learned and how much I had changed since the beginning of CFC, I sensed God's quiet voice telling me that writing a book might inspire others to serve in compassion ministry. The idea of writing a book was intimidating, especially since I had never desired to be a writer or considered myself having that particular talent.

A couple of years after that day, and before the annual women's retreat at my church, I prayed, *God, if you are serious about me writing a book to help others do ministry, then please, this weekend, somehow through a verse, a prophetic prayer or something, let me know if this really is Your will.* The first night of the retreat a basket containing verse references was passed around to all of the women. I chose a small folded up piece of paper from among the 700 that had been prepared and opened it to see the reference Habakkuk 2:2. I opened my Bible and read:

> *Then the Lord answered me and said: "Write the vision and make it plain on tablets, that he may run who reads it."* (NKJV)

I was undone. I felt that God could not have answered my prayer any more clearly. God was telling me to *"write the vision"*—the things I'd experienced and learned after many years of working with families in the inner city. Write it down in a book *"on tablets"* and *"make it plain,"* which I would do as I wrote from my real-life stories and with a spiritual mother's heart. And *"that they may run who reads it."* Perhaps my book could be a way of encouraging and supporting people to run their race, to answer the call to help others in need. God wants so many more people in our churches and in our communities to sign up, to get off the sidelines and join the race to address the needs of the hurting.

Another reason I feel called to encourage others to step out to help those in need is because of a trend I have noticed. Although the number of ministry schools has increased dramatically in recent years, seemingly so few of the passionate, God-loving individuals who graduate from these programs are actually becoming consistently involved in compassion ministry. I'm not sure why this is the case, but maybe my story and experience can inspire a few to step out. When people see the enormous need and the difference that can be made through acts of love and service, right in our own communities, more may choose to get involved in ministries that are serving the needy, the hurting and the marginalized. My goal is to instill confidence and provide guidance and resources for anyone with a burden to help those in need.

I approach this book from the perspective that God broke my heart with what was breaking His heart. Then He called me to run my race of service which was in the inner city. Even with all my mistakes and weaknesses, God still used me to help change the lives of several hurting families in the city. Maybe you too are burdened by the needs you see around you. I want you to know that if God could use ME to effect change, then I *know* He can use YOU!

Each of Us Can Make an Impact

While this book will help those in ministry—both those involved and those considering starting one—it is also meant to give practical direction and help to *any* Christian whose life is busy and full, yet, they still want to reach out to those around them. We are all called to love and help those in need. Using my twenty years of experience of working with needy and wounded people, I've got stories, Biblical teachings, a little bit of revelation, and some helpful advice that you might find useful. I learned most of this the hard way.

The stories in this book are true. In some cases, I have changed the names and identifying qualities of the people we served in order to protect their privacy. All other ministry leaders, teachers, and staff members are mentioned by their real names.

With my stories and in my discussion, I use examples and people from my own Spirit-filled Christianity worldview. But, as I have personally witnessed, God uses His people from every expression. I have great respect for the heart of so many others serving the poor, as exemplified by groups such as the Mennonite Church and the Catholic Charities. One man who helped Center for Champions in so many ways, including welcoming fifty rowdy inner-city kids into his beautifully designed, stain-glassed, stone church building, was a United Methodist Pastor. So please, if you find some doctrinal differences, don't throw the baby out with the bath water. There is much in this book that can help all people who are serious about helping the hurting.

I speak as a ministry worker but I believe that Christian social workers and others in helping professions may find much in the book that they could apply to their work, especially if they choose to start a compassion ministry or work with a Christian program. However, there will be nuggets of wisdom that may inspire even if they are working under the confines of a secular facility.

Section Topics

This book is comprehensive and covers the topic of becoming aware of the needs of others, as well as the many aspects of ministering to hurting people. If you take a glance at the table of contents you will see that there are six sections. Just a sample of the things discussed in the first three sections includes: recognizing the needs of the hurting, overcoming fears, and being equipped with kingdom foundational truths, such as that God is a good Father.

The next section addresses some of the difficult things that arise when working as a team and ministering to the wounded. I've read several books about ministry but few talk about personal struggles and what it's like in the trenches, day to day. I hope that my vulnerability will help others know that it's OK if they are experiencing some trying days. That's normal ministry life. It's not a reason to give up.

When one ministers to hurting people for a long time, compassion fatigue can become all too real, especially if the person in ministry doesn't take care of their own heart and feed their soul. Some of the things that help prevent burnout are worship, nature, joy, time with God in the secret places, and good friends.

Near the end of the book I share the joy of seeing lives changed and the heartache that we may endure when our efforts appear to fail. Finally, I share the sweet reward for being faithful to love "the least of these." That reward, in my opinion, is a closer and deeper friendship with Jesus. Overall, this book is loaded with a spiritual mom's wisdom for anyone wanting to walk this Christian life, helping others.

There's a world of people needing someone to give them a helping hand. We need the *whole body of Christ*, united together with hearts of love and committed to acts of service. Come on, let's do this for Him! Let's be His hands and feet to someone in need.

Let's love like Jesus!

... WHATEVER YOU DID FOR ONE OF THE LEAST OF THESE BROTHERS AND SISTERS OF MINE, YOU DID FOR ME.

MATTHEW 25:40

SECTION I

Deciding to Run the Race

CHAPTER 1

You Do Something

"Do Something" by Matthew West[1]

Turn Compassion Into Action

The TV was turned on to a news channel. We were amazed and appalled by what was happening in Los Angeles. The violence and mayhem started after four LAPD officers were acquitted of the use of excessive force in the arrest of a man named Rodney King. Someone videotaped the police kicking and beating him mercilessly. I cringed as I watched the injustice that was being revealed on the news station over and over. It seemed clear that they were abusing this unarmed man. The acquittal put the whole city in a state of rioting, looting, and violence. By the end, at least fifty-five people were killed, and a billion dollars of damage was done to the city. It was the spring of 1992.[2]

As we were watching the news that same day, they showed a white man attempting to drive his truck through the streets where a riot had started. Several black youths opened the driver's door and pulled him to the street, beating him over and over, almost to death. The news media caught the horrifying scene as it was unfolding. Finally, some brave black residents came out into the street, and saved his life by getting into his truck and driving him to the hospital. It was shocking to see what was happening. Many were outraged at those young men being so angry and violent. I was also alarmed and disgusted, but my heart was torn and drawn to consider what would cause them to respond that way.

My ten-year-old son was having some friends over that afternoon. Their eyes were glued to the television. Their facial expressions displayed shock and unbelief. I looked at them and said something like, "I know it looks like those guys are being really bad and they are. But you don't know what their lives are like. You don't know why they are so angry. They've had a tough life. It's so hard for them when people are so prejudiced against them and they don't feel like they get any justice."

After the boys left, I sat on the sofa, tears flowing. I could not stop crying. Today, when I think of my extreme reaction and the feelings I was experiencing that day, I realize that this event was stirring up my personal memories of growing up in Virginia during the 1950s-60s. I had witnessed the terrible racial prejudice that some of the friends of our family had endured. Often it had caused me to speak out in significant ways. Now, around twenty years later, some of the past was being stirred up in me. Living in suburban Pennsylvania, I hadn't thought about those experiences for a long time.

That day I cried out to God, *God, please, somebody has to do something!* And then I was shocked at what came next. I heard, not an audible voice, but a clear and direct inner-voice, in second person, undeniably God, stating rather emphatically, "YOU DO SOMETHING." I responded with, *What! Who, me? I don't know the first thing about the inner city.* The Lord responded, "You know about children." And I did. I had a couple of my own, and was the director of the children's ministry at a small church I was attending.

I decided to respond to God's directive. Since I knew nothing about the inner city, I took small steps towards getting involved. I asked around to see if anyone was helping inner-city children in Harrisburg. Someone directed me to contact Bethesda Mission Youth Center. I called, and signed up to volunteer one afternoon a week with elementary children in a crime-ridden part of the city. I also read books on racial reconciliation and urban outreach. After a few short months of volunteering, I was hired for a part-time job, teaching a program called *Confident Kids*[3] to the children and their parents.

Up to this time, I had only worked about two years as a social worker, when I first got out of graduate school, and most of that time was spent working in a nursing home. Then as my children came along, I was content to be a stay-at-home mom. But now, I was venturing into working with children and teens who lived in the inner city. I had a social work degree but my work experience was from 15 years before, and I had no training in urban ministry.

I was also very sick for a number of years with a condition called chronic fatigue immune deficiency. Some days, it was all I could do to make supper and invest in the lives of my own children, much less work outside the home. I really was one of the least likely candidates one might choose to work in this type of ministry. I hope that by telling you some of my personal story, you will see that if God could use me, He can certainly use you.

In 1977, when we moved to Linglestown, Pennsylvania, a suburb of Harrisburg, a neighbor told us to avoid going into downtown Harrisburg because of the danger. I, who grew up in a rural community, had no understanding of what the inner city was like. Their warnings made me petrified to drive down even the main thoroughfare (which, I later learned, was not very dangerous at all). So, when I felt God wanted me to actually volunteer in a much worse section of town, the real inner city, I did feel afraid at first.

I remember the first time I dropped a young girl off at her home in the housing projects. I sat in the car waiting for her to get inside her door. I kept looking all around to make sure no one was approaching my car. Then I felt like God said, "Hey, she lives here. You are afraid and can go home to your safe community, but what about her?" My eyes filled with tears—again—as they seemed to do so frequently in those beginning days. I'd drive through trash-strewn streets, pass buildings with graffiti and broken windows, and see signs of poverty and depression all around, all the while weeping and praying, weeping and praying. He truly was breaking my heart for what broke His heart! I soon found that the more love I felt for the people of the city, the less afraid I became.

That God-induced *heart breaking* led me to try to do everything I could to alleviate some of the pain I was observing in these neighborhoods. My efforts started off small—first volunteering and then a part-time job. Finally, in 1998, I co-founded a new ministry called Center for Champions of PA. For many years, I served as the executive director and as an officer on the board of directors.

In our daily after-school program at the Center we were addressing the needs of about 50 children and teens through many avenues: creative arts, dance, sports, academics, and spiritual activities, such as prayer and chapel time. Our strong spiritual emphasis set our program apart from many others. We read Bible stories and talked about the love of Jesus Christ. We described God as a good Father. (Most of our students did not even live with their earthly fathers.) We prayed for the children, and even encouraged them to pray for each other, the staff, and our volunteers.

Another unique aspect of our program was our strong emphasis on working with the parents of the children and teens. We made home visits, counseled parents, and accompanied them to hospitals, court sessions, student/teacher meetings, and way too many funerals. We also required the parents to attend our family dinners. This became a very successful part of our program. We had an average of 75 percent of the parents or guardians attending our monthly meetings. This continued year after year. These dinners provided an opportunity for the (mostly) single parents and children to actually sit down and eat together as a family, perhaps the only time that month. A special quality of these dinners was that families of several different races and cultures came together as one.

So, from that one small first step of volunteering a few hours a week, I was later able to help start the Center for Champions (CFC) program.

Here's a key to finding out God's call for *your* life. When you get a sense that God is calling you to do something, *take at least one small step toward that mission*, even if you have little direction or idea of where that will take you. I've prayed with various people who told me that they felt that God was leading them to minister in a particular country or to some needy population. But five years later I've met these same people and they haven't done anything toward that mission or for that population. They were waiting for more instructions, better timing, more money, or better circumstances.

The key is to just take one step toward the mission. Go on a short-term mission trip or volunteer occasionally with some population in need. ***Do something***. This will not only help you find out where God is leading, but can show areas for which you aren't suited and find little joy in serving. That's also an important lesson. You won't learn where God has called you, or even where you are not called to, by sitting and waiting for an ideal situation before you step out to serve others.

So Many Hurting Ones

Today's news is just as disheartening as the news broadcast in 1992. Reports on TV or on social media, words from our streets and in our schools, all reveal a world that is full of tremendous pain. As Christians, we have so much to offer to a hurting world. Will we rise up and address these issues with personal sacrifice and compassion?

Consider teenagers distraught and overcome with grief because a friend committed suicide, innocent women and children trapped in sex slavery, foster kids who have been abused, disabled teens needing programs to fit their unique challenges, single women who feel their only solution is abortion, elderly widows experiencing extreme loneliness, college students having no direction and losing hope, veterans with serious injuries or memories that refuse to be silenced, fatherless inner-city boys and girls, economically challenged prisoners who received a raw deal from our justice system, and refugees running for their lives, shell shocked, with tear stained faces.

Somebody's got to do something! YOU could be that one.

Let me tell you, as a social worker I have witnessed how our government solutions have often done little more than put on "band-aids," as they address a few of these needs. In some cases, government "solutions" have actually made the problems worse. A real tragedy of the twentieth and twenty-first century is that too many Christians have relegated their responsibility to love "the least of these" to the government. And yet, as believers we have so many answers to the heartaches driving the many problems.

WE MIGHT NOT CHANGE ALL THE WORLD'S SOCIAL PROBLEMS, BUT WE CAN CHANGE SOMEBODY'S WORLD

We might not change all the world's social problems, but we can change *somebody's world*. Too often, we think we have to start something *big* to be effective. That belief has stalled too many people from even trying. Even though Center for Champions is a small organization, I can point to a number of individuals whose lives have significantly changed since being loved and encouraged by the people who serve in that ministry. The current executive director has focused on increasing the number of mentors who interact with the children and teens. Just think how these one-on-one mentoring relationships can be life changing to a fatherless boy or girl.[4]

Studies have been done that show those programs that prove to be successful are often run by people who take their faith seriously and incorporate spiritual discussions into the activities and teachings of the program.[5] Small faith-based programs are often successful in helping individuals make better life choices and see lasting change. For example,

Teen Challenge, which has many programs for adults and teens who are addicted to drugs, is small compared to AA and other much larger programs that work with individuals dealing with addictions and substance abuse. Yet research documenting the progress of the participants has demonstrated that the Teen Challenge programs are producing good results.[6]

Big is not always the answer. Bigger programs mean additional administrative costs, require more buildings, and sometimes involve more bureaucracy. Some studies are showing that those programs that choose to remain small, while assisting and providing advice to others in ways to duplicate some of their services, can be very effective.[7] God might not be asking you to run some huge national ministry. (If He calls you to start a ministry and it grows and reaches multitudes, He will equip you to handle it.) For now, just take one small step and see where that leads you. You can make a significant difference in a few people's lives, if you determine to start taking some action to help hurting people. Can you see yourself doing that? With God's help, it's not hard to imagine.

Didn't Jesus tell us to go? *"Go out and train everyone you meet, far and near, in this way of life"* (Matthew 28:19, MSG). (Notice He didn't say go out and make converts.) What is this "way of life" that Jesus refers to? More and more believers have been gaining greater revelation about God's way of life. It includes the forgiveness of our sins and the power of forgiveness that we give to others. It entails the finished work of the cross of Jesus Christ. What great joy and freedom we have experienced when we realized our true identity in Christ! So many believers are starting to understand what it means to be true sons and daughters of a good, good Father!

The world needs to hear these life-giving, paradigm-shifting messages. We can't keep them to ourselves! We don't need to rehearse them over and over to the 99—the same group of people—when so many have never heard these messages, not even one time. They need what we've got! Sometimes, people just need a fellow human being who will hug them, pray with them, visit them, give them a ride to the store, bring them a bag of groceries, take them into their home for a few days, and speak life and hope to their hearts. *Can you do that?*

I'm asking you to seriously think about what breaks your heart. And, if you honestly don't know, or you are incredibly oblivious to the pain of others, start praying, **"God break my heart with what breaks your heart."** God is not looking for the amazingly brave and adventurous ones. He can do some remarkable things with the "little ole me-s'" as Randy Clark, [8] likes to call them.

In this very honest and open book, I share some of my vulnerabilities and expose some of my weaknesses, along with God's strengths, because I believe this will help you see that God can use *YOU* to make a difference, just as He used *little ole me.* I know that I was able to help bring hope, purpose, comfort, and practical help to several inner-city families. And, I have the joy and satisfaction of knowing that I answered the Father's call at that season in my life. I want that kind of joy for you.

Look Around: Can You Help One?

Not everyone has to change entire nations and open blind eyes, like some extraordinary missionaries we hear about. Not everyone is a powerfully anointed evangelist, winning thousands to Christ. It is fantastic that some are being used by God in these ways. It is helpful and inspiring for us to hear these speakers when they come to our churches. But we in the audience sometimes have mixed reactions to these speakers and their stories of the incredible ways God has touched so many through their ministries. A few people answer the call and boldly run up to the front, volunteering to be used by God and go to the ends of the earth. However, some let the stories "tickle their ears," with no personal reaction at all, because these feats of which they have just heard were so beyond the scope of their imagination of what they could ever do, that they determine it must not pertain to them. And, a few leave feeling pretty much like a "worm," believing they don't have the faith, and knowing they aren't brave enough and committed enough to do the things they have just heard about.

But, I'm here to tell you that some of us can embrace another response. Let the "laid down" lives of the amazing speakers we hear or read about inspire us to lay our lives down for even a few people who catch our attention as we go about our daily lives. Our response could be prompted by a feeling of empathy, as we listen to a news story highlighting a problematic situation. Or, it could be by something we observe on our drive to work. Maybe God is just asking you and me to help one family, one neighborhood block, or one needy group. We all can be used by God to help heal at least one wounded heart in some way.

God wants us to stop, if even just "for the ONE," as Heidi Baker,[9] a remarkable missionary, says. God wants us to open our eyes to the pain around us and see whom we might help. Jesus stopped for the One. In John 4:35, Jesus admonishes his distracted disciples with these words, *"You know the saying, 'Four months between planting and harvest.' But I say, wake up and look around. The fields are already ripe for the harvest."* Jesus said those words to his disciples, who were more concerned about whether Jesus had something to eat than about the life of the woman with whom He was talking. He had just spent his entire afternoon talking to one woman, who was of questionable reputation. (One whole afternoon was a lot of time considering that Jesus only had a three-year ministry.) He sat there by that well, prophetically telling her—without judgment—about her life, listening to her questions, and showing her what He had to offer. Jesus calls out to us, **"Wake up and look around!"**

Ask yourself. Who needs the love of God shown to them in practical ways? What's stopping you from seeing the needs and doing something to help? Are you confused about where to start? Are you afraid? Do you feel unqualified? Are you worried about having the necessary finances? I hope to address some of these concerns in the next few chapters.

Helping the "Least of These" is Being "Presence Driven"

My church has been blessed to experience revival and incredible times of worship. One term used to describe this type of church is being, "presence driven." We want to be in God's presence. We want to experientially know Him. We don't want to just sing songs about Him. We want to sing songs to God, being in communion with Him. I'm willing to drive great distances to be in a setting where the presence of God is tangible in the worship service.

One day a number of years ago, when I was at home listening to worship music I prayed, *"Lord, I want to feel and know more of Your presence. Show me Your presence!"* Immediately, I found my thoughts being turned to a section of scripture that I had not thought about or read for some time. It seemed to come out of nowhere. I knew it was God's answer to my request. He impressed on my heart some truths of what it can look like to be in His presence. Surprisingly, it wasn't a scripture about the elders falling to the ground as they worshipped in the temple. It wasn't about His heavenly glory. There were no references to the "eyes and wings" of which Ezekiel describes (Ezekiel 10:12).

Instead, I felt Jesus leading me to read Matthew 25:34-40. This is the parable where Jesus says, *"Assuredly I say to you, in as much as you did it to one of the least of these my brethren you did it to Me"* (NKJV). I sensed Him saying to me, "When you help the hungry, you are in My presence. When you give a drink to the thirsty one, you are in My presence. When you visit the prisoner or the sick person, you are in My presence." Jesus made it pretty clear that when we tangibly help those, whom He calls "the least of these," then we *are in His presence.* Let's purpose to become so filled with His love and His goodness as we commune with Him in worship that we overflow into the streets, taking His presence wherever we go.

Consider the goodness of God. He asks us to do something to help someone else, and yet, we always gain. We always benefit from giving.

What could be greater than being in Jesus' presence! It is so worth praying that prayer that I prayed years ago, "Lord, somebody has to do something!" And it's so worth answering, "Yes" when He says, "*You* do something."

Reflection and Action

LISTEN

- Listen to the song, "Do Something" by Matthew West.

- Reflect on the lyrics about what God's heart cry is and what is really important.

STUDY

- Matthew 25:31-40 (MSG), John 4:1-42 (NLT)

JOURNAL

1. As you look around you, is there a person or a group of people that tug on your heart?

2. Are you willing to pray and ask God to break your heart with what breaks His heart?

   If so, why not take a moment right now and ask Him to help you see with His eyes. Then, keep your eyes open, journal, notice others, and acknowledge divine circumstances. He will make clear opportunities to serve as you pursue His heart.

3. Is there something holding you back from praying this prayer or from stepping out to help someone? What is it?

WHEN WE TANGIBLY HELP THOSE WHOM HE CALLS "THE LEAST OF THESE," THEN WE ARE IN HIS PRESENCE.

More Needs to be Done

"Reckless Love" by Cory Asbury[1]

Being Jesus' Hands and Feet

Occasionally a worship song is released that seems to resonate with our soul. It becomes a joyous declaration of God's amazing love and goodness. "Reckless Love" [2] sung by Cory Asbury and released by Bethel Music is such a song. So many worshipers respond to this song by wholeheartedly belting out the dramatic chorus, which talks about how God lovingly comes after us. It speaks of a love so tenacious, so enduring, that it climbs mountains, kicks down walls, and tears down lies that we have believed.

We sing the words to this song, but what do they even mean? How does God come after us? Sometimes He orchestrates divine appointments or opens closed doors. Sometimes we experience an encounter with God where we sense Him speaking directly to our hearts. But, more often, He comes after us through other people.

Whose arms does God use to climb up that mountain? Whose foot does He use to kick down those walls—walls of shame, abuse, and pain? How does He tear down the lies, lies that we're not good enough, not forgiven, not loved? I'd like to suggest that since God has often chosen to limit Himself, and instead work through us, that many times He uses *our* arms, *our* feet, and *our* listening heart to accomplish His will. But He doesn't stop there. He wants every person healed, delivered, set free, and secure in His love. Helping someone reach that kind of maturity in knowing who they are in Christ takes time, discipleship, and unconditional love.

On the last night before His death, Jesus spent a significant amount of time talking to His disciples about loving one another. He even stated that their love would be the evidence to the world that they knew Christ (John 13:35). The world needs to experience this incredible audacious love of God that many of us have known. This is the kind of love that fights for us when we're down for the count. It's willing to take the effort to come looking for us, even if that means leaving the comfort of the familiar. Jesus tells the story of the man who left the 99 sheep and goes looking for the one. When he finds this lost sheep, he puts it on his shoulders, brings it home, calls his friends and joyously tells them how he found this precious one (Luke 15:4-7). The needy and lost ones will experience this kind of pursuing love when believers take up the charge to go looking and *loving like Jesus loved.*

I'm starting to see a significant number of believers willing to step out and take action to help more people. I find this movement encouraging. One of the things that was so beneficial during my time attending ministry schools was the times of outreach. Finding those people we felt God was leading us to pray for, was a gentle push out of my comfort zone. These encounters with people we didn't know helped me grow in boldness and be ready to see "what the Father might be doing" at any given time. Often, our encounters brought joy, comfort, and even sometimes physical healing to the person being prayed for. But I felt that in some cases the person we were ministering to needed *more* than we had offered. I hope to convince a greater number of people to be willing to provide "the more."

Providing "the More" to the Oppressed

One time I was with a group of ministry students sitting at a table in the McDonalds located inside a Wal-Mart. We talked and prayed together and then dispersed into the store looking for people to pray with. (In the New Testament Paul took his message and kingdom principals to the market place. Today, we have Wal-Mart. And, yes, we also try to make sure we buy something.) As we walked the aisles, we were inwardly asking the Father, *"Father show us who especially needs your love and prayer today."*

My attention was particularly drawn to one woman with long dark brown hair. I felt God had shown me a picture of a woman that actually looked a lot like her during our earlier prayer time. Approaching her lovingly, we explained that we were just walking around praying for people. I showed her some prophetic art that looked like a dark storm with swirls of golden light in the middle. I told her that this picture reminded me of someone coming out of a stormy situation into light. Then I asked if that spoke to her and if I could pray for her. She said it did, and was willing and appreciative.

As I prayed, I felt that she had been abused. I cautiously asked if she had been in an abusive relationship. She said that she had. In fact, she had just that week left an abusive relationship in another state and had moved to Pennsylvania to live with her sister, who was standing there beside her. Tears flowed down her face as she felt that someone understood her situation and cared. We assured her that God saw her, and especially wanted us to pray for her that day. We left knowing that this woman had encountered the Father's heart as we prayed. And for that, we were very grateful to have been a part of His plan for her life on that particular day.

But what if we could have offered even *more*? What if we had known a group of believers who had been trained in counseling or inner healing who would have followed up with her? Imagine if there had been a group of former ministry school students living in our city who had chosen to live together in community. What if someone had taken the necessary steps to incorporate and form a non-profit compassion ministry with multiple resources to assist abused women (and perhaps men) in significant ways? Then, I could have given her their card or their number.

And she would have had the opportunity to receive inner healing prayer, wonderful teaching about her true identity, practical resources, and guidance toward finding a job and housing—everything that she might need to start her life over.

Domestic violence is a huge problem in the world. One in three women and one in four men in the United States has been physically abused by a partner or relative.[3] If you have ever been at a women's retreat where the speaker asked those who have been physically or sexually abused to stand, the number is astounding. Praying with these women during an outreach or at a church meeting is a great start, but they need so much more. Who is providing "the more"?

Providing "the More" to the Addicted

On one occasion, I accompanied a group of ministry students to the inner city. We prayed for a number of people, who seemed blessed by the experience. The students I was ministering with were elated. But as I drove home, I could not get one young mother out of my mind. My eyes filled with tears as I recalled her young children and how she had been clearly inebriated or high on something. I wish I had known a group of believers with the skills and resources to help individuals struggling with substance abuse. She needed more than our blessing prayers that day. She needed a community of praying and knowledgeable believers to help her address her addiction and get her life back on track. We had only given her a little taste of God. We had not offered any tangible services to address her needs. I know God well enough now to know that these tears were not just my own; the Father was breaking my heart once again with what breaks His heart.

There are too many people who are struggling like this woman. Addiction, especially opioid use, is increasing in epidemic proportions in the United States.[4] The Center for Disease Control reports that, "Between 2002-2013, the rate of heroin-related overdose deaths nearly quadrupled, and more than 8,200 people died in 2013."[5] Some people get hooked on opioids after first taking pain pills for an injury. Others turn to these drugs to ease emotional wounds. Then they turn to heroin because it is more readily available. These people need more than medical and psychological help. They need the unconditional love of God that can heal the underlying causes. They need the power in the name of Jesus Christ to break the chains of addiction. Believers who know their identity in Christ and have a heart ready to give unconditional love without judgment could do so much good. Together with other believers, they could surround these hurting ones with a great support system.

There is a tremendous need for more consistent, hands-on ministry. There are individual believers, some who are retired with years of wisdom, some who are ordinary church members with willing hearts, and others, who are ministry school graduates, that are well-equipped to provide this additional help to a variety of hurting people. As they say, "Yes," to His call, the Father will direct steps, open doors, and provide divine appointments. He will guide this process because it's so dear to His heart. I hope that this book will inspire readers to think about the various needs in the world and their ability to address them with God's help. An army of believers, who are in love with Jesus, really CAN make a difference in this world, if only they will respond to His call.

Providing "the More" Toward Lasting Healing

In recent years, it's been refreshing for me to see many believers taking steps to get out of their comfort zone and pray for healing. As our faith has risen, we have seen many notable miracles and people restored to wholeness. Personally, I have had the blessing of being used by God to pray for several women who were unable to conceive. What a joy it was, a short time later, to receive pictures or messages of their beautiful babies. I personally believe the church's willingness to step out and pray for healing has increased because of the wonderful teaching and example of men and women like Randy Clark, Bill Johnson, Heidi Baker, Georgian and Winnie Banov, my pastor Charles Stock, and many more. In addition, many prophetic speakers, such as Bob Hartley and Shawn

Bolz, have increased our desire and boldness to prophetically pray for others. They have shown us that this can be a tremendous way to share the heart of the Father.

While offering prophetic and healing prayer often leads to miracles and incredible encounters, I am saying that we could go further. *There is a significant lack of people taking this compassion for others to the next logical step.* The world needs a community of believers who will stay around and be there to help, not just for one outreach or one time during prayer ministry on a Sunday, but the other days, week after week—discipling, teaching, helping, and loving wounded souls.

> THERE IS A SIGNIFICANT LACK OF PEOPLE TAKING THIS COMPASSION FOR OTHERS TO THE NEXT LOGICAL STEP.

Both one-time encounters, where we pray with someone for a need such as a miraculous healing, and consistent actions, where we help provide for spiritual and physical needs, are vital kingdom tasks. However, there needs to be many more believers willing to provide the consistent actions, "getting in the trenches" so to speak. Just think of how many more needy people could be helped. Oh, how this will touch the heart of the Father! I can sense His smiling face as if He is saying, "Finally, someone is allowing their heart to break with the things that break My heart. Finally, they are willing to DO something compassionately and consistently. I've been waiting for this day."

An abused woman needs to know she is unconditionally accepted and loved by God. Suicidal teens need to know that their lives are precious and there is hope. Along with prayer and encouragement, they may need help from a Christian trained in mental health issues. A drug addict needs to know that receiving Jesus Christ into his heart is more satisfying than anything else, as well as help to find the strength to face and overcome the pain that the drugs or alcohol is covering. Some have been miraculously delivered of addiction in one day. But others have recovered over time and required assistance from the love and support of fellow Christians. A pregnant teen needs to know more than the fact that abortion is wrong. She needs to know God loves her and is the giver of life to her child. She needs to know that if she chooses not to have an abortion, she won't be alone. Others will be there to help her.

There are so many societal needs and not enough Christians taking practical actions to address them. Wouldn't it be great if a group of ministry school grads, or friends in a church, would take steps toward finding additional people who also have a passion to address a particular need? Some could make an announcement at a church or others could send out an email request to various ministry schools' alumni list. They could ask if there are qualified people who would be willing to move to the same location, with the goal of starting some type of ministry work. Perhaps some in the group would be willing to go back to college to get a degree in social work, counseling, education, business administration, or human service. Taking courses and getting some type of certification can add legitimacy to one's ministry. During all those years I was a stay-at-home mom, I never used my social work degree. But it became incredibly helpful when I started Center for Champions.

God's Word Sheds Light on True Ministry

Eugene Peterson's translation of the Bible, the Message, seems so poignant concerning our need to respond to others with compassion and action. Let's consider what James, the Lord's brother, tells us as interpreted in this version:

> *But whoever catches a glimpse of the revealed counsel of God— the free life!—even out of the corner of his eye, and sticks with it, is no distracted scatterbrain but a man or woman of action. That person will find delight and affirmation in the action.*

Anyone who sets himself up as "religious" by talking a good game is self-deceived. This kind of religion is hot air and only hot air. Real religion, the kind that passes muster before God the Father, is this: Reach out to the homeless and loveless in their plight, and guard against the corruption from the godless world (Jas. 1:25-27, MSG).

And here:

Dear friends, do you think you'll get anywhere in this if you learn all the right words but never do anything? Does merely talking about faith indicate that a person really has it? For instance, you come upon an old friend dressed in rags and half-starved and say, "Good morning, friend! Be clothed in Christ! Be filled with the Holy Spirit!" and walk off without providing so much as a coat or a cup of soup--where does that get you? **Isn't it obvious that God-talk without God-acts is outrageous nonsense?** *(Jas. 2:14-17, MSG; emphasis mine).*

I know from experience that deciding to take action truly does help people in difficult situations; and lasting change results from long-term investment in people's lives. As believers, we can help more effectively, when we address the "body, soul, and spirit" or the physical, emotional, and spiritual needs of others. Most hurting people won't receive these deep truths through just one encounter. They won't receive it from reading a tract. Hurting people need a community of believers to surround them with the love of God, words of wisdom, and a helping hand. Deep wounds sometimes take a process to heal. This process should involve loving relationships, bringing light where there once was only dysfunction and darkness.

Reflection and Action

LISTEN

- "Reckless Love" by Cory Asbury

- Consider how God pursues you with His love. How can He use you to go after others with that same love?

READ

- Luke 10: 25-37, Luke 15:4-7, Luke 15:11-32, 2 Corinthians 10:4-5 (NLT), Galatians 6:1-2 (MSG), 1 Thessalonians 5:11

JOURNAL

1. What is one way you could make a practical difference and provide "the more" type of help in someone's life today?

2. What is a way that you could get involved with an organization or ministry that works to meet a societal need where you feel burdened?

3. Who around you have a similar passion and would go with you to address a need? How might you find those individuals?

DECIDING TO TAKE ACTION
TRULY DOES HELP PEOPLE IN
DIFFICULT SITUATIONS.

CHAPTER 3

The Fatherless Crisis

"Break Every Chain" by Will Reagan[1]

A Social Crisis of Epidemic Proportions

Hakeem stood in the doorway, his head down and his lip jutting out with an air of defiance. He had been sent to my office because of getting into some fights that day during our after-school program. Sending him to me, the executive/program director, was the last resort. One of my roles, especially in the beginning years, was to be the person dealing with discipline issues (and frankly, I hated that part of my position). I told Hakeem to come in. He entered, dragging his feet and with an angry look on his face. Unfortunately, anger seemed to be part of his persona already and he was only about eight years old. He was upset about something almost every day.

"Hakeem, why are you so angry?" I asked. (Honestly, sometimes you just don't know what to say. I wasn't a professional child therapist. I just wanted to help this boy, if I could, and stop the fighting.) At first, he didn't say anything. And then, when I pressed the point, he said with great confidence, "I'm gonna go to prison, just like my dad!"

I was shocked. I was not expecting that answer at all. My first reaction was to say, "Oh Hakeem that's not true. Don't say that. That is not your destiny. God has a good plan for your life." His face softened a little. I asked him about his father, "So, when was the last time you saw your father?"

Tears started to well up in those big, beautiful, brown eyes, and he let out a little whimper, "Three years ago."

By now my heart was aching so much for this little boy, but I tried to be the professional "therapist" in the situation.

So I asked, "Hakeem, if you could see your dad what would you like to do? Go to the park or play baseball or something like that?"

He was quiet and then he looked up into my face and said, "I just want to look at him."

That was all my heart could take. I scooped up this little boy and put him on my lap and just rocked him. (The social work boundaries went out the window. I was a mother at heart.) He and I had a good cry.

I wish I could tell you that Hakeem's was an unusual situation. But this was the norm. Many of the children in our program had a father who was in prison or had been in prison. Several had never seen their fathers at all or had no contact with them. Only a few knew their fathers and got to see them. On a rare occasion, a child might actually live with their own single father. I could count the number of children living in their home with both biological parents on one hand—no, actually, with one or two fingers.

It's clear that there is a foundational social issue in America that is at the root of many problems in our nation today—it's not gun control, drug abuse, teen pregnancy, abortion or domestic violence. These concerns, and so many more, are often symptoms of the issue of *fatherlessness*. The numbers of physically or emotionally absent fathers are staggering. The National Center for Fathering (NCF) reports the following: "More than 20 million children live in a home without the physical presence of a father. Millions more have dads who are physically present, but emotionally absent. ***If it were classified as a disease, fatherlessness would be an epidemic worthy of attention as a national emergency...*** The impact of fatherlessness can be seen in our homes, schools, hospitals and prisons...In short, fatherlessness is associated with almost every societal ill facing our country's children"[2] (emphasis mine).

The NCF website lists some notable statistics about individuals experiencing various societal problems and how many of them are not living with a biological father—90% of homeless children, 71% of teens who get pregnant, 71% of drop outs, 63% of teens who commit suicide, 85% of youth in prison, 70% of those in correctional facilities, 71% of adolescents who abuse substances, and 44% of those living in poverty.[3]

Just how prevalent is this problem of fatherlessness, as defined as children not living with their biological father from birth or later on in life? *The Moynihan Report Revisited* states, "In the early 1960s, about 20 percent of black children were born to unmarried mothers, compared with 2 to 3 percent of white children. *By 2009, nearly three-quarters of black births and three-tenths of white births occurred outside marriage.* Hispanics fell between whites and blacks and followed the same rising trend"[4] (emphasis mine). In addition, the statistics of the numbers of children living without a father present in their lives are disheartening. The US Census Bureau in 2012 reported that 57.6% of black children, 31.2% of Hispanic children, and 20.7% of white children are living apart from their biological fathers.[5] Unfortunately, fatherlessness is not only a problem in the United States. Around the world there are many fatherless children living in orphanages, or centers, as they are usually called today. Others are found in numerous refugee camps and still others are living on the streets.

God is a Father to the Fatherless

The statistics are daunting, and could seem hopeless, but Christians have reasons for hope. We may not be able to solve all of society's problems, but we do have a message to help the fatherless ones. From God's Word, we offer the life-giving message that *God is a Father to the fatherless* (Ps. 68:5).

Jesus revealed the heart of the Father to the world. Numerous scriptures, including Romans 8:15, tell us that God adopts us into his family. He is a Father that loves us unconditionally, even when we make mistakes.

This is so clearly illustrated in Luke 15, where Jesus tells the story of the prodigal son and his forgiving father running to him with arms open wide. God is real. He is a loving, amazing Father who hears our prayers. He will never leave or abandon us (Heb. 13:5). The world needs to hear this! Who's willing to go tell them?

At the Center, it took time to get this message across to the children. The after-school program was, after all, only a few hours of their afternoon. There were many other factors affecting the lives of the children other than the afterschool program. I'll be honest, we didn't always succeed in bringing God's healing to everyone's scars. I still remember the day when one of my Center comrades called to tell me that Hakeem, who was now sixteen, had been arrested and was at Dauphin County Prison. He had stopped coming to the Center several years before that, and I had heard that he was getting into trouble. I responded, "Oh no, not Hakeem!" I crumbled down beside my sofa and cried, envisioning the angry little boy who just wanted to see his father. I remembered his words, and realized, sadly, now they were coming true. He did go to prison just like his father.

> SOMETIMES JUST LISTENING, JUST TEACHING THEM TO FORGIVE WAS LIFE CHANGING.

Fortunately, that was not the case with everyone. There were many instances where we were able to bring emotional healing to the father-issues they were experiencing. Very few of the people we worked with had a healthy family situation or a church family where they could find emotional or spiritual healing. Sometimes, just listening to them and teaching the children and the parents to forgive was life changing.

One evening, we had a group meeting with the mothers of the children at the Center. I wanted to learn more about the fathers of the children in our program. I decided to first ask the mothers about their own fathers.

That question opened up a flood of emotion. Great sobs and anger and stories of abuse poured out of their hearts. I realized we had to start by addressing their pain. We never even got to the question about their children's fathers.

We discussed the detrimental effect of holding anger and judgments against their fathers and, in some cases, their mothers. They learned the power of forgiveness, and how it breaks the chains that were binding them to the offenses. Some of the parents received more extensive inner healing prayer sessions from my co-worker and a local pastor. Some of them were really starting to see some breakthrough.

One night at the Center, we asked a black pastor to come to our teen program to address issues some of the teens were having regarding their absent fathers. This was significant because a majority of the children at the center were African American. He walked to the stage and talked about God as a loving Father. Then, he asked any teens who had issues with their own fathers to come on stage and he would pray for them. He stood "in proxy" for these nowhere-to-be-found fathers. He asked for forgiveness, and the teens responded and forgave him. He told them that he loved them, and gave them a father's embrace and a father's blessing. It was a really powerful evening. The youth were visibly touched. I do believe some of these fatherless teens had areas of their hearts supernaturally healed that night.

You may wonder how someone can stand in place of a person who wounded somebody else. Personally, I have seen the amazing effects of this type of inner healing prayer while ministering on a prayer team. It's a great tool Christians have to help bring healing to hurting people, even if the person who committed the offense is not repentant or even alive. Once a person has chosen to forgive their earthly father, or another offender, God can completely erase a pattern from their families. They don't have to repeat the sins of their fathers.

At my church, I know two of the best fathers I have ever met. Their biological fathers were poor role models, making life at home extremely difficult. By the time they were teens, their biological fathers were absent from their lives. These two men came to the Lord in their late teens and early twenties. Soon they had children of their own and God was able to help them forgive and not repeat the sins of their fathers. They actually became the total opposite from what they had experienced in the way they related to their family. Interestingly enough, God blessed each man with three wonderful daughters. Their daughters are now beautiful young ladies who love God, love others, and have an outstanding sense of confidence from being loved and honored by their fathers and their Father God. God's love can truly break any chains.

The Father Speaks

An amazing experience concerning the topic of God's father heart occured in chapel one day. The staff had just gone to some training by a man named Brad Jersak. He taught some useful and enlightening ideas about ways to help children hear God for themselves. He wrote an interesting book called *Children Can You Hear Me? How to Hear and See God.*[6] That day at chapel, I decided to talk about how much God loved the children as a good Father.

Knowing their family situations, I looked out at the precious children and said, "Some of you don't live with your fathers."

Then one seven-year-old boy, who was right upfront leaning on the steps of the stage, raised his hand. "Ms. Denise, I don't live with my father."

"I know, Sean, I'm so sorry," I said.

Sean was a unique child. He had first come to the Center when he was about six years old. He would daily get into fights or say something mean to someone. We tried to talk with him about his behavior. We told him that Jesus loved him and wanted him to love others. He would respond in sort of a growl, "I hate Jesus. I love the devil."

We knew a little about spiritual warfare and demonic oppression. Sometimes, I'd speak softly and tell the demons to be quiet. Please don't be concerned by my words if this is out of your spiritual paradigm. It's reasonably apparent that little six-year-old children do not naturally hate Jesus, or naturally love the devil, nor do they growl when they talk.

He would seldom sit through an entire chapel service without having to be removed because he made so many distractions. So, this day, when he was sitting up front at the stage, I was a little bit leery as to what he might do to disrupt things. But—praise God—that day the presence of God was so thick, and perhaps our faith so high after going to that seminar, that the enemy was defeated.

After speaking, we asked all the children to find a place in the room, get quiet, close their eyes, and let Jesus speak to them. We put on soft music and waited. After about five or ten minutes, we asked children to share what they had heard. We were blown away by some of the things God revealed to their hearts—many were things that we had not even discussed.

One girl said, "I was lying on the floor in the middle of a dark room. Then Jesus came in the room, flipped on the light and reached down and picked me up. He said, 'I adopt you!'"

A boy said he saw himself going from door to door talking about God.

There was a tall handicapped pre-teen girl in our program who had the mental capacity similar to a five-year-old's. She said she saw Jesus pushing her on a swing. Now, I never said one word about swings and Jesus, but we all knew that swinging was one of the things this girl loved to do more than anything else. Hearing her say this brought tears to our eyes. We were elated, and honestly sort of surprised. It was so powerful to hear how God had directly spoken a Father's heart to these children.

But the most miraculous statement of all came from Sean. I was sitting on the stage and he sort of scooted up beside me and tugged on my shirtsleeve.

"Ms. Denise, Ms. Denise," he said with a twinkle in his eye and an air of excitement.

I looked down, wondering what this was about. "What is it?"

"Jesus spoke to me," Sean replied definitively.

Honestly, I was shocked to hear this from him. I looked at him and said, "What did He say to you?"

"Jesus said He wants to come into my heart."

I was thrilled. I spoke with him some more about what Jesus had done for him, how He had died on the cross to save him. I told him He wanted to be the Lord of his life and what that meant. I asked Sean if he believed these things and he said he did. Sean prayed and asked Jesus to be his Lord and Savior.

From that day on, Sean never again said that he hated Jesus and loved the devil. The revelation that God is a good, loving, accepting Father, who does not abandon us, was life changing for this young, fatherless boy. Years later, I was filled with joy to see a picture of him getting baptized at a local church.

There is a world full of fatherless people all around us. They are not all in the inner cities. Some are abused women. Some are successful, but lonely, businessmen. Some are refugees who have seen the horrors of war. Some are troubled teens in rural America. Maybe you are one of them. Fortunately, it's not a hopeless situation. Isn't it great to consider that we Christians have the privilege to introduce them to the Father who never leaves, never abandons, and heals wounded hearts?

Reflection and Action

LISTEN

- "Break Every Chain" by Will Reagan and United Pursuit

- Fatherlessness seems like such an insurmountable problem, but the power of the finished work of the cross, ministered in the name of Jesus Christ and demonstrated with actions of love has the power to break every chain that takes root in our lives and even in society.

READ

- Psalm 68:5, Romans 15:8, Luke 15:11-32, Hebrews 13:5

JOURNAL

1. Did you grow up in a home with a physically and emotionally available father?

2. If you had a present father, how did your father influence your life? And if you did not have a present father, how did his absence affect your life?

3. How do you think a revelation of God as our loving Father can fill in the gaps of fatherlessness?

THERE IS A WORLD FULL
OF FATHERLESS PEOPLE
ALL AROUND US.

SECTION II

Overcoming Obstacles

CHAPTER 4

God Can Use the Timid

"Take Heart" by Joel Houston/Hillsong United[1]

Immobilizing Fear

I sat behind my computer. Hesitantly, I pressed the *send* key. Click, the email describing the new Center for Champions (CFC) program was sent. I thought to myself, *That's it. It's official! We really are going to start this ministry.* Then suddenly my hands got sweaty, my breathing shallower, and fear, immobilizing FEAR, gripped my thoughts. I had just written this email to several people who knew me well. I told them that my friend and I were starting an inner-city ministry to help not only children, but also their parents. I guess I felt that by sending this email there was no turning back.

I had worked part-time for a few years at an inner-city, after-school ministry. But now, starting a completely new 501(c)(3) non-profit ministry would be taking my working in the economically challenged areas of our city to a whole new level. My thoughts were swirling with questions. How would I handle the added responsibilities involved in leading this kind of ministry—the legalities, the funding, the staffing, the building?

Although these things had not been my concern in my part-time work, that job had introduced me to some of the difficult scenarios one encounters in urban ministry. As staff, we dealt with angry students, broke up fights, and often found it an extreme challenge to get the class to do homework or listen to teachings. One time, as a hardened teenage boy was walking out of the building, he looked me straight in the eyes and threatened me with these words, "I'm going to 'pop' your son." In

43

other words, he was saying he was going to *shoot* my teenage son, who had volunteered that day. I burst into tears. Was I committed to doing God's will? Yes. Brave? No.

I left that job after four years due to health reasons and other concerns. When I left, I wasn't sure I'd be doing anything like that ever again. But now, only two years later, in response to God breaking my heart for what breaks His heart, I was committing to do much more than I'd ever done before.

I knew what I was committing myself to do. I saw the cost very well. As I wrote this email to friends, announcing the startup of this ministry, I was thinking about all that it would involve. I started to freeze on the inside, my mind telling me that I was crazy to even consider doing this. In my heart, I knew that it was something I really didn't know how to do, didn't have the strength to do, and maybe didn't even really want to do.

That evening, I dragged myself to our small group meeting and told them how afraid I was feeling. This wonderful community of believers had heard my dream of launching CFC, cheered me on, and knew what I was planning. Every member was behind it 100%. So, they surrounded me with prayer, lovingly placing their hands on my head and shoulders. Some felt I had been attacked by a *spirit of fear*. Others prayed for faith, confidence, and peace. That night I slept well. In the early morning hours, when I was barely awake, I had a vision or you could say a clear mental picture. This was not something I had experienced very often and was totally unexpected, but so profound:

> *Jesus and I were walking through Hall Manor (an inner-city housing project). We were knocking on doors. But as I knocked, it was Jesus' hand superimposed over mine, as if my hand was literally being His hand. We skipped houses, as if we were specifically targeting certain ones. Then, I saw all these lovely faces of children pressed against the glass doors of our church. Their big brown eyes had expectant looks that said, "Let me in, now!"*

In the next scene, we were inside the main children's church room and other people were reaching out to the children. I didn't see the faces of the people, just their hands reaching out to the kids, and Jesus' hands superimposed over their hands, as with mine. Then I looked and there was Jesus sitting in the corner, with such a hilarious smile, such appreciation, such gratefulness on His face that someone was finally taking care of His kids. He let out an enthusiastic and loud, "Yes!" with His hands pumping the air like some basketball player who had just hit a three pointer at the sound of the buzzer to win the game! And my heart melted in such love and such willingness to do anything that would make My Jesus THIS happy! "Okay, Jesus," I said, "Yes, Yes, Yes! I'll do it for you."

That day, *love cast out my fear.*

Over the years, some really precious people have come up to me at church, and said things like, "You're my hero." First, I was shocked, then extremely humbled, and finally a little bit amused at the thought. *If only they knew the real, not-so-brave, not-so-confident me.* I want to eliminate misconceptions people might have regarding fear and its connection with doing ministry. I think some of us, especially those of us sitting in the audience at a conference or a church meeting, believe that only the really confident, brave, and maybe even a tad adventurous people go into serving in a compassion ministry. I've seen fears and doubts keep others from following through on dreams and callings. I want to shout this out with the authority of my experience:

YOUR FEARS AND YOUR INSECURITIES DO NOT DISQUALIFY YOU!

Your fears and your insecurities do not disqualify you!

No Shame in Being Afraid

There is no shame in feeling fear. Many think it reveals a lack of faith, or weakness, if we experience fear and doubt about our ability to do something God is asking us to do. This feeling of shame caused me to feel that I was not God's first-choice leader for starting CFC. For many years, I felt that someone wiser, braver, and more confident was the *right* person, but they just hadn't answered the call.

Now, looking back over the 16 years of ministry, I am a little bit wiser. I realize that God did use me significantly to start and keep this ministry going for many years until the right time came to pass the baton. I realize that God did call *me* to do this, and I was exactly the right person for what He called me to do.

Certainly, God has used the rare thrill seekers or the super confident, but remember this book is addressing the "little ole me-s."[2] Often, God isn't looking for the bravest and most confident. He especially likes using the weaker ones because they know it is only in His strength that they are accomplishing anything. He is just looking for people who will trust Him and take the steps needed to go forward, even if their knees are knocking, and they have to remind themselves to breathe. I love how Joyce Meyers words it in her book, *"DO IT, AFRAID"*![3]

The degree and cause of fear differs for each of us depending on our life experiences and temperament. What makes one person afraid may seem like nothing to someone else. Each of us has our own comfort zone. On my worst days in the inner city, days when I had teens fighting, or people cussing me out, or perhaps a day when I personally messed up and didn't handle a situation very well with staff or the children and parents, I'd come home, run up my stairs, and go into my prayer/guest room.

In my overly dramatic manner, I'd drop to my knees sobbing, *God what are you doing to me? I can't take this anymore.* But then I'd say, *But thank you Lord, that you didn't call me to go to Mozambique. Thank you that I can serve you and still take a hot shower. I can sleep in my own comfortable bed, with no mosquito nets.*

I know that some of you might think that prayer was quite petty, but for me, that was my way of saying yes to staying and doing inner-city ministry right here in my hometown. It often felt like I was already way past my limits. So, this prayer was my way of reminding myself that I could do this. God wasn't asking too much of me. Going to Mozambique would have seemed like torture to me with my already weakened immune system and trouble going to sleep. Plus, I don't even like camping in the good ole USA, if I'm being real.

God knows us each intimately, and calls us on different paths. For example, a really precious young lady, that I extremely admire, worked for CFC for about a year. She did decide to go to Mozambique for a short-term mission trip and ended up staying long-term. Eventually she married a man from Mozambique and had several beautiful children. For several years they were the directors of the Pemba mission base for Iris Ministries. I'm sure that, at times, she feels out of her comfort zone, but she seems to be thriving and really enjoying living there with her family. It works for her. It's where God called *her* to go.

God Will Make You Brave Enough

I firmly believe that if God calls you to do something, He will give you the strength and even the bravery, to do it. Trust your Daddy God. He knows you better than you know yourself. He will be with you all of the way. As I prepared to start CFC, God encouraged me with the verses Isaiah 41:10-13. Verse thirteen is a great one to memorize: *"For I, the Lord your God, will hold your right hand, saying to you, 'Fear not, I will help you'"* (Isa. 41:13, NKJV).

God is like a loving father who will help us and hold our hand! I still remember my own natural daddy's strong hands. God is a wonderful Father. So, let me encourage you. If you have some idea, some inkling that God is calling you to do something that seems too big, too difficult for you, *He will not ask you to do it alone.* He will hold your hand.

In the 1980s, and early 1990s, as I have mentioned, I was afraid to even drive down the main streets of my city—Harrisburg, Pennsylvania. Picture me, as a young woman in my slightly run-down Chevy, a base model with no automatic locks, stopped at a red light. I would see an African-American youth in a hoodie, standing at the light, waiting to cross the street. This alarmed me and I would panic. Frantically, I would bend over the seats and twist myself all over the car to lock all the car doors, imagining this man might try to get into my car or do something. (I don't know what, but in my mind's eye, it couldn't be good!) This is the honest truth. This *was* me.

After I knew that God had called me to do ministry in the inner city, and had gotten a little bit of experience, I was no longer afraid. I'd walk down the worst streets known for crime and shootings by myself (in the daytime—I wasn't stupid), and knock on doors. I went to remind parents that we really did want and expect them to come to our parent dinners. I'd talk to drug-dealing boyfriends about taking care of their children.

Sometimes, I'd have to stay alone at the Center after work hour to finish up a project. I was not afraid, even though it was in the heart of one of the worst districts. I'd pray, *God, I think tonight I need my body guards!* A sense of peace would settle over me, as I actually sensed that angels were with me. I'd quote a familiar verse like Psalm 23:4 (KJV), *Yea, though I walk through the valley of the shadow of death, I will fear no evil, for thou art with me.* (It's funny how our brains revert to the first Bible version we learned when we are in a potentially stressful situation.)

I have often heard my pastor, Charles Stock, quote this statement (often attributed to Corrie ten Boom) while teaching:

The safest place to be is in the center of God's will.

So many times, I'd recite that thought and, by God's grace, peace would settle over me. My fears would have to go. God doesn't always call us to "safe," as in not very dangerous places, but there is a peace and security in knowing that we are living our lives doing what we know God called us to do. However, this statement did give me faith that God would be with me and I felt I'd be okay. I never got mugged. I don't remember ever having things stolen from me while working at the Center. (My car got stolen at my church, but that's a story for the next chapter.) You'll be amazed at what you too will be able to do when you answer His call.

One late afternoon I was walking on a street in a particularly bad section of town. We were walking our CFC kids back from visiting the local fire station. It was one of those winter days when it gets pitch dark by five pm. A teenage African-American boy in a hoodie, which was pulled down so far, I could hardly see his eyes, walked right up to my face. I had a short moment of hesitation wondering what was about to happen.

Then in a deep, urban-slang voice he said, "Was-sup, Miss Denise?"

I looked closer and I realized this young man, now towering over me, had been a student in our after-school program a number of years earlier when he was just a little boy. I gave him a big hug. As I walked away, I chuckled, and pondered in my heart just how far I had come from being afraid of youths in hoodies at stoplights. Now, not only was I no longer afraid, but I had been given the gift of knowing some of them personally, and deeply loved them.

Our level of fear and how we respond is influenced by our life experiences and temperament. One thing I love about our Father God is that He meets us where we are. He knows how we are made. Like a good father, God knows just how far to nudge or challenge His child to be all they are destined to be. I have experienced God calling me out past my comfort zone, but never has He asked me to do something that would be traumatizing.

God didn't ask me to start a nonprofit ministry reaching 50 children when I was a stay at home mom, knowing nothing about the inner city. First, He called me to volunteer just one afternoon a week. Then, I worked twenty hours a week as a group leader in an after-school program for almost four years. Finally, I felt the call to actually start and manage an urban ministry. Even David first killed a bear, and then a lion, before he faced Goliath. God's not going to push you off the high dive if you aren't even comfortable with your face in the water. Oh, trust Him dear ones. *He really is trustworthy.*

God Uses Unlikely Leaders

The Bible is full of unlikely people that God used to do amazing things. In Judges 6-7 God used the most unlikely person to do an amazing feat that we are still talking about today. Honestly, this story could have a comical side to it. If the few lines from the first chapter were set in today's lingo I think it might possibly have gone something like this:

Angel of the Lord says, "Hey G, my man, you're awesome. You're a hero!"

Gideon's reply, "Huh, you talkin' to me ... What! Hero? No way. My family's the lowest of the low and I'm the lowest in the family. I can't rescue anybody ... Is this really happening? You better prove it to me."

I don't think the angel talking to Gideon was Gabriel (most likely not). If it were, Gabriel would probably have been thinking to himself, "He better shut his mouth before I shut it for him!" After all, we know how Gabriel responded to Zechariah when he questioned his message (an unscriptural, non-theological paraphrase of Judges 6:11-17).

I'm having a little fun with this scene, but the reality is that God had incredible patience toward Gideon. The Lord proved to him over and over that He would be with him. *Take courage* in this account. God used Gideon, who had an extremely low opinion of himself and did not believe God could call him to such a purpose, to free a whole nation.

So what oppression breaks your heart? What do you notice that others don't? Is God drawing your attention to address this need? Do you wish you could help, but are afraid because it seems so beyond your abilities? Consider these words from Bill Johnson:

> WHAT OPPRESSION BREAKS YOUR HEART? WHAT DO YOU NOTICE THAT OTHERS DON'T?

Our authentic dreams from God cannot be accomplished on our own. That is a sure sign that a dream is too small. We must dream so big that without the support that comes through favor with God and man, we could never accomplish what is on our hearts.[4]

If the desire of your heart is to do something in a significant way to help others, I hope you are encouraged that God will be with you every step of the way. Trust me, I know what I am talking about. He will faithfully hold your hand and help you in countless ways. Come on my friend. *If God can use me, I know that He can use you.*

Reflection and Action

LISTEN

- "Take Heart" by Joel Houston and Hillsong United

- This song reminds us that we can take courage in knowing that God has overcome all our fears, our failures, our troubles.

READ

- Isaiah 41:10-13, Judges 6-7, Psalm 56:3-4, Psalm 23, Psalm 4:8, Joshua 1:9

JOURNAL

1. What are your greatest fears in reaching out to help people?

2. What type of ministry do you think you'd like to serve in but are hesitant for various reasons?

3. If this chapter has helped you realize that God can use you in spite of your weaknesses, what next steps could you take toward becoming more involved?

CHAPTER 5

Conquering Fear

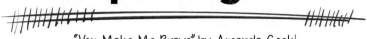

"You Make Me Brave" by Amanda Cook[1]

Tenaciously Resist Fear

We've laid the foundations to understand that fear is nothing to be ashamed of, and that God can use us in spite of our fear. But now, I want to make it understood that fear can be one of the biggest obstacles you will face—and you must conquer it. In 1932, the United States was experiencing a deep economic depression. Many people were out of work and some were even starving. A number of people were beginning to wonder if things were hopeless and began to panic. Franklin D. Roosevelt expressed this idea regarding fear at his first inauguration:

> *So, first of all, let me assert my firm belief that the only thing we have to fear – is fear itself.* [2]

Many stop short of fulfilling God-given destinies because they rationalize away their calling, not recognizing the root issue is fear. You must tenaciously resist and conquer fear because it can immobilize you and prevent you from accomplishing God's plan for your life. Fortunately, God has equipped Christians—through awareness, prayer, the Holy Spirit, the Word of God, and love—to resist fear and be victorious.

Awareness of the Enemy's Weapon

Apprehension, hesitancy, and lack of confidence are all aspects of fear. When these feelings start to control us and keep us from doing things we desire to do, especially for God's kingdom, then we have a problem.

Fear is one of Satan's greatest weapons against the believer, but we don't have to be defeated by his tactics.

Fear can actually be so strong that is becomes a belief. But it is a **belief in the negative**, a belief that the very thing one is afraid of will happen. It then attracts the enemy and negative consequences. *"What I always feared has happened to me. What I dreaded has come true"* (Job 3:25). Likewise, *"The fear of man brings a snare, but whoever trust in the Lord, shall be safe"* (Prov. 29:25 NKJV).

This reality gave me the will to conquer the compelling fear that was affecting many areas of my life. In a somewhat odd way, it made me "afraid to be afraid", and gave me the gumption I needed to not allow fear to rule me. I realized crippling fear was something I could not ignore or accept. It had the power only because I was giving it. That's not to say that I am now an extremely brave person. I am not. But I know what to do with fear when it starts to control me.

Fear can be natural. It is reasonable to be afraid of being harmed, especially if you are caught off guard in the middle of a dangerous situation. But then there are unreasonable fears—fear of *potential* harm, fear of failure, fear of financial difficulties, and even the fear of man's opinion. These have stopped many a good person from obeying God. He still loves them, but they lose out on much of what they could have done for His kingdom. More importantly, they lose out on having a special intimacy with Jesus that they would have gained from the experience of obeying and trusting Him. On top of that, many needy people are harmed because no one was brave enough to enter their sphere to bring the love of the Father and practical assistance.

If Satan can't stop you from getting saved, he can at least stop you from being used by God to touch others' lives with His love. When I contemplated beginning the inner-city ministry, the enemy told me things like, "You can't do this! You don't know how to run a ministry.

You're not healthy enough. You're not a minority or a single mom. They won't listen to you."

I had to choose to not believe him. And you will have to choose the same thing. Don't let the enemy talk you out of what you know God is asking you to do. God did use me, and others like me, to reach many who came from different backgrounds. When we allow God to fill our hearts with the Father's love, our weaknesses and our differences don't matter. *Love speaks its own language. It transcends cultures, economics, and life experiences; it conquers racism and prejudice.*

Prayer Quiets the Storms

Some feelings of fear are actually caused by the enemy sending a "spirit of fear" on top of our own weakness. I was being attacked by a spirit of fear the night I went to the home group meeting and asked for prayer about starting CFC. The Bible tells us, *"For God has not given us a spirit of fear and timidity, but of power, love and self-discipline"* (2 Tim. 1:7). So, the believers had all the authority to tell this oppressing spiritual attack to leave. And it did. Peace entered where a storm had raged.

Worry and anxiety can become fear. Paul gave great advice in how to overcome worry by telling us to pray instead of being anxious (Phil. 4:6-7). Taking your concerns in prayer to God not only helps counter fear, but can bring peace and calm to our minds and our spirits. Other people praying for us and with us is essential, too. I'm so thankful for those who cared about the Center and prayed for my personal concerns and the ministry issues on so many occasions. If you are going into ministry, it's really important to have people who will pray for you.

The Holy Spirit Imparts Boldness

Embracing and receiving the inherent power of the Holy Spirit is another key in overcoming our fears. Before the day of Pentecost, fear caused Peter to deny his Lord. It wasn't that he didn't know that Jesus was the Christ, the Son of God. Peter is the one who made that declaration. It wasn't that he was disillusioned because Jesus was not going to bring a revolution. No, the only thing that caused Peter to deny the greatest man he had ever known, the man he loved so much, was fear. That's the power of fear. And after Jesus was crucified, the disciples were still afraid: *"[T]he disciples were meeting behind locked doors because they were afraid of the Jewish leaders"* (John 20:19a).

Yet, 50 days later, after they were filled to overflowing with the Holy Spirit on the day of Pentecost, Peter stood up and told a large public crowd of people that they had crucified Christ and they must repent (Acts 2:1-40). Later, he and John got arrested and were told not to speak in the name of Jesus. Observe their boldness now, *"But Peter and John replied, 'Do you think God wants us to obey you rather than him? We cannot stop telling about everything we have seen and heard'"* (Acts 4: 19-20). An angel helped them get out of prison and return to the other believers. Together they prayed for more boldness and for more signs and wonders in the name of Jesus. Then the whole place shook, and they were renewed with a filling of the Holy Spirit (Acts 4:23-31). Being filled to overflowing with the Holy Spirit changed Peter and the disciples from fearful men to ones walking in amazing boldness. It can change us too. I know being filled with the power of the Spirit, changed my life in so many ways, especially with regard to overcoming fear.

There were a few evenings when I'd be walking to my car in the parking lot that was located on one of the most crime ridden streets in the city. I'd focus on how God was with me. I'd remind myself of the power and the authority that I knew God had given to me and start praying in the Spirit. When you pray in the Spirit, it's a very tangible way of reminding yourself that God is indeed with you and in you. You are speaking to God, praising Him and praying about situations of which you don't even know. Romans 8:26-27 states, *"For example, we don't know what God wants us to pray for. But the Holy Spirit prays for us with groanings that cannot be expressed in words."* And, it is another way to build your faith and strengthen your courage in the face of fear. *"But you, beloved, building yourselves up on your most holy faith, praying in the Holy Spirit"* (Jude 1:20 NKJV).

Authoritatively Declare the Word of God

Another powerful weapon against fear is knowing and speaking the Word of God! We must face fear with a certain tenacity, giving it some *attitude*. Showing some attitude is not just for the naturally bold ones. It can be cultivated by experientially knowing the Word of God and believing what the Bible says about who you are in Christ. Sometimes, you even have to speak out loud and speak directly, "Fear, in the name of Jesus Christ go! Get out of my thoughts, my body, my heart, my home, this situation!" The Bible says, *"Resist the devil and he will flee from you"* (Jas. 4:7 NKJV).

Isn't this what Jesus did with every temptation from the devil, when He was confronted in the wilderness? *"Get out of here, Satan,"* Jesus told him, *"For the Scriptures say, 'You must worship the Lord your God and serve only Him.' Then the devil went away and angels came and took care of Jesus"* (Matt. 4:10-11).

Renew your mind with His Word. *"You are of God, little children, and have overcome them, because He who is in you is greater than He who is in the world"* (1 John 4:4 NKJV). You have all the authority and all the power you need to tell FEAR to go. Learn scriptures and then "kick the enemy in the teeth," so to speak, with the Word of God, pressing past your doubts and fears.

One of the actions that best helped me to overcome fear was when I started writing down scriptures that pertained to fear and memorized them. In the Reflection and Action section, at the end of this chapter, I have listed many. Take the time to seriously study these scriptures and search the internet for other scriptures, listed in multiple versions. Now, is a key time to memorize some of these scriptures, because in the middle of a scary situation, you need to have the Word going through your mind to combat the fear.

A loving and bold minister named Andrew Shearman taught that sometimes when we're under attack, we need to recognize the authority given to us by Christ Jesus, and tell the enemy, "Hell!" "NO!" An interesting play on words, but the point that *we're not going to take it* comes across magnificently.[3] In Matthew 16:18b-19, Jesus said, *"[A]nd upon this rock I will build my church, and all the powers of hell will not conquer it. And I will give you the keys of the Kingdom of Heaven. Whatever you forbid on earth will be forbidden in heaven and whatever you permit on earth will be permitted in heaven."*

Once, my car got stolen at my church, which was located in the inner city. We had just started going to this church, but I knew in my heart that this was where God was calling us. The devil's scheme was to discourage us from going to that particular church, but I was not going to let him succeed. An unusual tenaciousness rose up in me. I reminded the devil that he had no claim to any of my property; and that God had given me authority over him (Jas. 4:7, Luke 10:19).

While boldly marching around in my basement, I declared that the van would be found and everything that was inside (including valuable items like a guitar, amp, and cd player) would be recovered. Then, for some reason, I added these words with force, yelling, "And at least one of the guys who stole this van will get saved." It was a God moment. I felt His righteous indignation. I'm not always that authoritative.

A man we knew who was ministering to some troubled youth thought that there was a possibility that some of them had stolen it. He commented to them about how awful it was that someone had stolen my car and the items inside when I was a person who helped inner-city kids.

It wasn't long before the police found the car. And gradually, somehow the youth "found" everything and all was recovered. Even my cd player "just appeared" in his van.

Years later, I met a man who was visiting our church. He turned out to be one of the guys who had stolen my car. He said that six months after our car incident, he was in jail for stealing cars. He told me that while he was in the jail Jesus appeared to him in his cell. He became a Christian. *Drop the mic! That's what I'm talking about*! You have authority over the devil. Don't forget it. Use it.

Love Conquers Fear

Finally, the most powerful way to overcome fear is to be led by love. Scripture tells us that *"perfect love casts out fear"* (1 John 4:18 NKJV). Love compels many to go into very challenging situations. A beautiful young lady I know went into the heart of the Congo and then into war-torn areas of the Middle East helping refugees and others in need, armed only with a guitar in hand and a heart full of the love of Jesus. She explains it this way, "It is falling in love with Jesus that compels us to go to the crazy places to seek the treasure that is hidden in darkness! It is what sustains us and gives us courage to speak on behalf of those who can't!"[4]

It was my love for Jesus, and wanting to obey what He was calling me to do, that made a way for me to overcome my fears of the inner city. *As I've said before, the more love I felt for the people of the city, the less afraid I became.* Do what you know God is calling you to do, even if you feel worried and afraid. Do it because you love Him. Do it because you love His people. Love truly does overcome fear!

> THE MORE LOVE I FELT FOR THE PEOPLE OF THE CITY, THE LESS AFRAID I BECAME.

Reflection and Action

LISTEN

- "You Make Me Brave" by Amanda Cook and Bethel Music

- This song reminds us that God helps us change. As the realization of His love washes over us, our fears subside and we become brave enough to do what He is calling us to do. Love overcomes our fears and no fear can stop the promises of God.

STUDY

- Write down verses that deal with overcoming the enemy and your authority in Christ. Write down scriptures that particularly speak to you regarding the subject of overcoming fear and anxieties. Choose several to memorize.

- James 4:7, Ephesians 6:11, Luke 10:17-20, Matthew 28:18-20, Matthew 4:1-11, Romans 8:37-39, Hebrews 2:14-18, 1 John 4:16-19, 1 John 4:4, Philippians 4:6,7, 1 Corinthians 12:7-11, 1 Corinthians 14:39

JOURNAL

1. Would you consider yourself a very brave person or not very brave? Why?

2. What has helped you in the past when you felt afraid? What have you learned from this chapter to help you grow in overcoming fear?

3. Is God asking you to do something that you feel hesitant or afraid to do? What is it? Contemplate—is He worth it? Are those precious needy ones worth it? Read Matthew 16:24-26. Is our life our own or are we called to follow Jesus' example, losing our lives to gain His kingdom?

CHAPTER 6

Finances and God's Faithfulness

"Do it Again" by Elevation Worship[1]

Not My Faith but His Faithfulness

It was 1999. I was driving home one evening after attending a meeting with a few enthusiastic and visionary young men. I was there to network with them and discuss their mission to create a program using basketball and mentors to help urban youth. I listened to the description of their five-year plan—purchase a building, reach a large target population, and raise significant funds. I was not about to burst their bubble, but inwardly I thought their expectations were too high for just starting out.

As I drove home, my thoughts turned toward what I felt were unmet expectations after our first year at Center for Champions. Twice, I had high hopes of getting grants that seemed to fit what we did perfectly. One grant gave us a bland, thanks-but-no-thanks, reply. The other never responded at all. A professional athlete came to the Center to interact with our kids one day. When he received a several million-dollar contract, I was sure we'd receive some type of contribution, but none came.

So, this night, my thoughts spiraled into discouragement. My eyes filled with tears as I mumbled to myself, *I used to be like those guys. I used to be so gung-ho. I thought we'd do so much. And, I used to think we'd have all this money to do it, that it would just come in so easily.* I complained out loud, "It's not like that, God, is it? No, it just doesn't come that easily, does it?" I got no answer.

I got out of my car, wiping off the last drops of disappointment from my chin. I went inside and talked to my husband. He said, with sort of a smile on his face, "There was a large envelope stuck in our door tonight for Center for Champions. I saw it when I opened the door. Here it is."

The envelope was bulging with something. I looked inside and there were mostly twenty-dollar bills. I counted $20, $40, $60...$2,000 total! There was $2000 in cash for the Center anonymously stuck in my door! I was floored. I wondered who on earth gave us this much, and in cash. Since then, I think I figured it out, but they never admitted it. As the reality of this gift settled in, I started jumping around, praising God, laughing, and crying. What a good God!

Do you ever wonder if God gets pleasure out of surprising you with blessings? I honestly think He loves to bless us and exceed our expectations, sometimes in outrageously extravagant ways.

That night began my journey of seeing the faithfulness of God to sustain the Center for Champions. Some on our board would say that I was a particularly strong woman of faith. But honestly, I disagree with that description of me. I was just a woman desperate for God to intervene and therefore I leaned on Him. It was not about me, it was about God and His Faithfulness. My biggest method for fund raising was prayer. But this was not passive prayer without action. As a staff, we'd pray about what to do in a situation. Then, God often directed our steps, showing us a place to at least start.

In considering whether to embark on the mission that God puts on our hearts, we often feel that finances will be a roadblock. Sometimes, people don't know even where to begin to find the funding. God is faithful, however, to provide for the dreams He places in your heart. Prayer is the key. He will guide and show you different ways of finding support for the ministry work you are doing. I saw so many ways He guided all of us at the Center in finding needed resources.

Keys to Finding Resources

There are a number of ways to find the resources you need for ministry. But first you should always pray. Then you should take action. There are many things you can do: get an education in a related field, work, ask for donated items, reach out to like-minded believers and others who have a passion for the needs you are addressing, hold fund raisers, apply for grants, and use social media to raise awareness of the work you are doing in your ministry. None of these ideas are more spiritual than the other, as long as you are approaching raising funding with prayer, and listening to the Father's guidance.

Now, I'd like to flesh out these fund raising ideas with some specifics.

PRAYER

Prayer is first and foremost the most important action you can do in finding support. God likes us to ask and depend on Him. What can I say, He's a good Father. We prayed all the time for God's help in funding our ministry. We had our personal times of prayer, but also had special times of staff and volunteer prayer. We sent out prayer requests to special prayer partners. The Center kids prayed for funds. We even took piles of newsletters and placed our hands on them before we mailed them out, asking God to bring our needs to the attention of the ones who would receive them.

Once, when our van was totally falling apart, we posted in a newsletter our need to buy a used 11 passenger van in very good condition. We prayed over the newsletters hoping that this need would catch someone's attention. One man who received our newsletter just happened to have received an inheritance. He and his wife had been praying about where to send a tithe of that money. As they read about the good things happening at the ministry and saw that we had a great need for a van, they decided that this was where God would have them give their money. They sent us a check for $12,000 to buy a nice, used 11-passenger van. You should have heard the loud screams of joy that erupted from the office the day we opened that mail.

BENEFITS OF EDUCATION

Sometimes God provides resources before we even realize it. Years before, God had guided me to get my master's degree in social work. By the time I needed to make the decision to go after a masters, I was more interested in doing mission work than becoming a social worker. But God opened the door so wide leading me in the direction of continuing my education, that I felt I had to go through it. Once I finished my master's degree, I worked a few short years in a nursing home and then became a stay-at-home mom for fifteen years. Through all that time, I questioned why I had "wasted" the time and money to get that additional degree.

When we started the Center, however, that degree made a huge difference. It gave some legitimacy to my position when we applied for grants or foundation funding. It made it possible for us to have about 25 social work and human service interns over the years that I was the executive director. Interns were like having FREE staff. And even more than the financial benefits, the interns brought their unique skills and dedication. As their supervisor I was able to provide helpful advice, especially to Christians pursuing a social work degree. In addition, our agency benefited tremendously as we networked with Messiah College.

Having a college degree comes in handy. If you have the resources and the aptitude for academics, I highly recommend getting a degree in some area that pertains to working with people. That said, however, God uses people with all kinds of talents and skills.

WORK

I think when people decide to do ministry they automatically think they need to abandon their jobs. But in the beginning years, you may have time to do both ministry and work. The Apostle Paul's life was characterized both by times when he was working as a tent maker

(Acts 18:3) and times when he received total support (Phil. 4:15-16). Working is a godly kingdom attribute. You can form relationships and represent Christ on the job. I include work in this discussion because so many young people seem to think the only way to get support for their mission is to write letters asking others to support them. That may be an important aspect of funding, but not the only one.

Some couples support a ministry with one spouse working a paid job and the other doing most of the hands-on ministry. This happened in my case—and I always felt that my husband was such a significant factor in the work at CFC. Sometimes a ministry requires both of you to be involved full-time. In those cases, you will need to look for other income options. You could consider possible sources of income from a small home business, or even some type of investments. Or, you might find all of your needed income from raising support.

Even though my husband had a good job, and thus I did not need a salary, the others who worked at the Center did need their paycheck for monthly living expenses. So, as the executive director, one of my responsibilities was to make sure we had the resources to pay our bills and our staff. Some years that meant raising $200,000. That was a real stretch of faith for me, but I knew God as faithful. He proved this time and time again. I estimate that, over the sixteen years I was with CFC, at least 1.5 million dollars came in. Now that's God's miraculous provision, especially since I was not a "marketing" type of person in the least.

FINDING SUPPORT

I had no marketing skills and hated fundraising. Fortunately, in my first year, a young pastor told me, **"Don't think of it as**

> DON'T THINK OF IT AS FUNDRAISING. THINK OF IT AS FRIEND-RAISING.

fundraising. **Think of it as** *friend-raising*." That was the best advice anyone could have given me. In the process of looking for support for our ministry, I met so many precious people with a heart for inner-city children and teens, or for the single moms with whom we worked. Some were successful business people. Some were hard-working couples. And some were individuals who simply gave $20 a month. All made important contributions that allowed us to have the resources and staff to do the work of the ministry.

It's extremely important to let your supporters know how valuable they are to the mission. Remind them that they are reaching needy people who might not be helped without their support. *I always think it's a shame when business people, who work really hard and give so generously, don't realize how important they are.* Remind them that they are actually doing ministry with their gifts. Encourage your supporters. Keep in touch with them through newsletters, emails, Facebook, Instagram, YouTube, your website, etc. Invite them out for lunch. Listen to them. Be genuinely interested in their lives. Let them see the investment they have made as you share stories of those with whom you are working.

When I saw fundraising as "friend-raising," finding the funds needed was not as burdensome. It actually became a great way of connecting with people of like heart and mind. There were so many wonderful ministries in the world and yet these people had chosen to give to Center for Champions. It was quite humbling. Never take it for granted. Always remember that it's an amazing blessing to be the recipient of people's giving.

FUNDRAISERS

Some ministries have golf tournaments, banquets, 5K runs, etc. We found our golf tournament to be successful in providing needed funds. However, let me give a word of caution about fundraisers. Think through the staff time involved and the overall profit of doing the event. Don't waste time on lots of small fundraisers. They are not always time well spent. Instead, consider spending just one evening connecting personally with one family or one person who supports your vision. They may decide to write a check that covers the entire amount you would make with a small fund raiser, or they may connect you to someone else who will.

GRANTS

Don't depend heavily on grants to finance your program. The website NonProfit Hub states, "Most recommend around 20% of your funding be grant-based; any more than that, and you risk sinking your organization if a key grant falls through."[2] I have watched several good ministries be ruined by depending too much on grants. One had to completely close down. The other had to abandon their original mission in order to comply with the grant requirements.

Read the fine print of any grant with which you are presented. Many grants from government or corporate sources may say that anyone, even religious organizations, can apply. But then you find as you read the proposal that they limit your ability to talk about Jesus Christ, or to have Bible lessons or prayer. Don't take a grant that limits your spiritual time to one small segment of your program. Just don't do it. There are many social programs, but the world needs to know the Father God. There are wounds that only Jesus can heal.

Also, beware of grants that require you to spend lots of time doing one program that they are promoting, especially if that program steers the ministry away from its original mission.

You must be the one who sets the direction, not the grant. It helps to have a clear vision, asking, "What need is God calling us to address at this particular time?"

At the same time, remain open if you sense God leading in a different direction. For example, for years Center for Champions held an after-school program helping 50 children, four days a week. Now, the new director is focusing on smaller groups of youth and finding one-on-one mentors for them. It's been fantastic to see how this new focus is helping the youth. This change was instituted to follow where the new director felt God's leading, not to receive funds for some particular grant.

Therefore, keep your mission and your target population defined. Be diligent to hold fast, even if others don't understand why you aren't adding a food or clothing ministry or something else. You know the vision God put on your heart; remind yourself of that mission often.

MANAGING MONEY

I personally believe that receiving people's hard-earned money is a holy thing. We have a responsibility to operate our ministry *with the highest integrity*. Be sure you have someone with experience in bookkeeping handling your finances. And if your ministry grows and you start having additional staff people, consider hiring an accounting firm to handle payroll, taxes, and a year-end review. Don't depend on that cousin or friend who is "good with numbers." Protect yourself and your ministry by hiring someone who really knows what they are doing.

Trusting in God's Faithfulness

From the beginning of our ministry, we decided that we would tithe ten percent of what was given to us, unless it was a designated grant. We specifically gave to other ministries that helped families and children because that was also our mission. We provided the money for resources and several cows for a wonderful ministry called Umuryango Children's Network. They help orphaned and/or street children, and other needy children in Rwanda. We sent funds to a school in Haiti. Twice, some of our staff and teens actually went to Haiti to minister. What a joy it was providing financial help to other ministries! Honestly, our decision to give to others helped my faith when we needed funding. It was our way of declaring that God was our provider and that we were totally dependent on Him. We trusted in His faithfulness.

It wasn't hard for me to trust that God would provide. My earthly father was generous to the poor and to his family. I think the fact that I never really lacked what I needed made it easier to believe the money would be there when required. Once, when I was 16, my dad and I went shopping for a used car. My eyes landed on a used, base model, metallic-blue convertible Camaro. I thought, *Oh, my goodness, what a beautiful car.* I'm sure that wasn't the kind of used car my dad had in mind, but he got it for me anyway. If my earthly father provided for me, over and above what I needed, then I knew my heavenly Father certainly would take care of the needs of the ministry that He called me to do.

For others who have known lack in their lives, trusting God to provide might be very stressful at first. But, over time, as you experience God's provision, you will see that God is trustworthy and you'll learn to rest in His faithfulness.

Build up your faith by writing down all of the ways He has gotten you to this point. Rehearse His faithfulness and goodness in your mind. Trust Him when it seems you might not have enough. Many months at CFC we operated month to month with just enough to pay the bills. Often at the last minute a check would come in the mail, someone would hand us a check at church, or we would get awarded funding from a small foundation. Keep in mind that God's timing is not always our timing. And He knows what is best for your ministry.

God Proves Himself Faithful

I remember that there was one particularly difficult time, however, when we actually didn't have enough money to pay all of the staff members. We paid about half the staff—the ones who needed it the most. Then I told the bookkeeper to give away the little we had left to ministries that we usually supported. We didn't have enough left to cover the other bills anyway. I told him to just keep $100 left in the bank, so as not to bounce any checks. And then we prayed.

This was about six years into the program. Up to that point, we had always had enough to pay the bills and all the staff. To say I was disappointed would be an understatement. I was depressed and didn't know what to do. The thought went through my mind that if God wasn't providing now, perhaps it was time to close down. Three days after I informed the staff of the situation, we still had not received any checks.

One morning during this time, I was so despondent that I told God I wasn't getting out of bed until He told me what to do. Different ideas to address our financial situation started coming to my mind. I got up and started to take some action. It turned out these ideas were answers to my prayers. I called a church that supported us monthly, and asked if they ever gave additional one-time donations. It just so happened that their once-a-month mission committee meeting was going to be that night. They said they would discuss it. Also, I called my own church and asked if they would consider giving something extra.

While we were going through this challenging financial time, my son came home from college. I told him how concerned I was about our financial needs. He suggested that I listen to a CD by Jason Upton called *Faith*. I prayed and listened to that CD over and over for several hours. The songs were so faith-building. (This is one example of why it is so life-giving for those in ministry to make a playlist of encouraging songs.) I loved these words in the song "Gideon":

> *I lift my eyes toward the heavens*
> *I tune my ear to your command*
> *Help me boast in my condition*
> **You're the God and I'm the man**[3] *(emphasis mine)*

Soon, I was shouting out the words to that song with all my heart. I knew that I had no way of coming up with the money we needed— but that God could do anything. That song turned my faith around, reminding me to trust in God completely.

Soon after, I heard that the mission committee had decided to send us a check for $2000 over and above their monthly donation, and that my church was also sending an additional check. The bills and the staff got paid, but we had a credit card bill of $600 that had just arrived in the mail. We didn't have the money at that time to cover this, nor did we operate our ministry on credit.

I said in a matter of fact way to God, *What about this?* Later that day, I went over to my church and decided to clear out an old mailbox that we no longer needed. When I got to the mailbox, I was surprised to find a letter there. Somehow, there was a check sent over a month before from a church that occasionally supported us. The check was for $600. We got exactly what we needed!

Frankly, I think that was the last time I really worried about money for Center for Champions. From then on, when my bookkeeper would call with those familiar words, "Denise, I'm looking at paying payroll and next week we will not have enough to cover that and our payroll taxes," I'd take a breath, then sort of chuckle.

Then I'd say, "Well, let's see what God is going to do this time." Those were not the words of a "strong woman of faith," *but the words of a surrendered daughter, who had experienced the faithfulness of her Father.*

Reflection and Action

LISTEN

- "Do it Again" by Joel Houston/Hillsong United

- "Gideon" (Valley/Victory) by Jason Upton

STUDY

- 2 Corinthians 9:1-15, Philippians 4:10-20, Ephesians 3:20, Luke 6:38, Malachi 3:10

JOURNAL

1. Have you ever had an experience where God provided for a particular financial need? If so, write some of these experiences down and keep for future reference.

2. In what other ways has God shown Himself faithful in your life?

3. Search the scriptures for verses about God providing for our needs. Write them down and keep them in a folder along with your record of God's past financial and resource provisions. Someday, you might need to revisit that folder to build your faith.

SECTION III

Equipping Yourself for Serving

CHAPTER 7

Do You Know God is Good?

"Good, Good Father" by Housefires!

My Daddy's Lesson

When I was a child, riding snuggled up against my daddy in the front seat of his pickup truck was always the highlight of my day. Daddy worked long hours, mostly 7 a.m.- 6 p.m. I loved the chance to be with him. I remember one evening I sat squished between my dad and Viola, as we drove her home.

Viola helped my mother weekly with ironing and house cleaning. She was a hard-working woman who had endured a harsh life of poverty and prejudice. One of the greatest difficulties she dealt with was living with an abusive husband. A large scar ran down the side of her neck where he had cut her one time. Mom would tell her to leave him, but where would she have gone? How would she have lived? As an African American woman living in the South in the 1950s, her options were limited.

We rolled along, bouncing as we hit the ruts and potholes, on that old, country road leading to the area where Viola lived. In those days, in my rural county, most of the local African American people lived in a community made up of small, shack-like one or two-bedroom houses. They had no running water or any other of the modern facilities available at the time.

Driving along that day, Daddy pointed over to a single, tiny square house back up in the woods that looked exactly like the houses I had seen in Viola's neighborhood.

"That's where your uncle Eddie lives," he said.

I was totally confused. In my innocent, five-year-old childish manner, I said, "Daddy, Uncle Eddie can't live in that house. That's a colored person's house." (The term *colored person* was an acceptable term in the 1950s.)

Daddy didn't say a word and neither did Viola. She got out of the truck and walked to her little house. Then my father looked at me with sad eyes, and said quietly, but with a seriousness, "Neecey, you shouldn't have said that. You might have hurt Viola's feelings."

I was caught off guard; stunned actually. Big tears welled up in my eyes and gushed down my cheeks. I am sure I thought, *What did I do? What did I say?* I had no idea that saying that my uncle couldn't live in a colored person's house would hurt Viola's feelings. I did not understand the implications of what I said or the tensions of the racial issues in the South at that time. But I did know that my daddy was telling me that something I said had hurt Viola. I liked her and sure didn't want to hurt her feelings.

That day, I learned something from my earthly father that stuck with me for the rest of my life. I learned that what we say matters. I learned to respect all people regardless of their station in life, their race, or their beliefs. I learned that I needed to be sensitive to the fact that everyone had feelings and act accordingly. My father and mother modeled acceptance and generosity to others. Even though we lived in rural Virginia in the 1950-60s, where racial prejudice was rampant, they made it clear that all people were important and loved by God.

The Father's Voice

As I look back now on that day I rode along to Viola's house, I realize that besides learning how to treat people, I learned something else equally important. I learned what a kind father's voice sounded like, even when he was correcting me. Daddy did not yell at me. He didn't call me a "stupid idiot" for hurting her feelings. He lovingly showed me how my actions had hurt someone else. He didn't harshly condemn or disown me. He gently reminded me of higher standards.

Once, after going to my boyfriend's prom, I got home extremely late. I hadn't called anyone. (No cell phones in those days.) I guess I hoped no one would notice. He noticed. The only thing he said was, "Neecey, you came home pretty late last night." Amazingly, that was all I needed to hear to be more conscious of what I was doing.

I LEARNED WHAT A KIND FATHER'S VOICE SOUNDED LIKE.

Honestly, the fact that I took my father's words to heart surprises me now that I think about it. I am a pretty strong-willed person. However, I so loved him and never wanted to disappoint him. Our motivation to please God should be the same. We obey and follow His lead out of our love for Him, not because we feel like worthless sinners or fear punishment or judgment.

Knowing what a loving Father's voice sounds like has often helped me distinguish God's voice from the condemning, accusatory taunts of our enemy, the devil. It isn't hard to distinguish between the lies and the false accusation of the enemy when you are so familiar with the authentic, *encouraging voice* of the Father.

Although my father helped me understand the heavenly Father more easily, one doesn't have to have a father like I did to know the Father heart of God. The Word of God continually tells us of His patient love for us. Even in the Old Testament, the psalmist wrote:

> *He does not punish us for all our sins; he does not deal harshly with us, as we deserve ... He has removed our sins as far from us as the east is from the west. The LORD is like a father to his children, tender and*

compassionate to those who fear him. For he knows how weak we are;
he remembers we are only dust (Psalm 103:10, 12-14).

Keep this in mind as you go about your life and as you help others. If you know God unconditionally loves you and gives you grace, you will, in turn, treat others that way, too. I haven't always been an expert at that, but I've learned over the years and have tried to do better in this area. God will direct your steps.

The Holy Spirit will bring conviction, at times, as you grow in your walk with God. But it never comes in a threatening, disowning, or angry way. Any condemning thoughts bombarding you are from your life experiences, your own negative self-talk, or the enemy of your soul.

God Has No Sinister Side

Suppose I told you that at my father's service station he allowed his mechanic to install new brakes incorrectly on a minivan, knowing that the family would get into an accident. My father's reasoning for messing with the van being so their prodigal son would be so concerned about the family getting into an accident that he would return to his family to help them out. You'd say, "What! Your dad was a Dr. Jekyll and Mr. Hyde! He was a monster!"

Of course, my earthly father never did anything like that! But my point is that Christians sometimes talk about God, our Father, as if He brings sickness for a higher purpose or brings natural disasters to kill people in judgment. How many times have good Christians said things like, "God didn't cause the accident, but He allowed this tragedy because He knew it would bring the family back together." Or, some might say, "His ways are higher than our ways. We just don't understand why He did this." Why do so many people assume that God causes the tragic things to happen?

Honestly, it sickens my soul when people blame God for everything that happens in this world. If my decent human father would never conceive of doing such a thing, how can we attribute evil to the most loving Being in all the world, our *Abba* Father. Some seemingly good people talk about God as if He is a psychopath. This is maligning our Father God's reputation.

This particularly concerns me because as we minister to a hurting world, we need to have a clear view of the goodness of God. Why should they listen to us if they feel God hates them and has brought destruction in their lives? It's important to consider how to encourage people who are going through difficult situations.

There are times when we go through some difficult experiences and God doesn't intervene. We can't always definitively know the "why" in every situation. There are things beyond our scope of knowledge in the spiritual realm that may come into play. But it seems clear from a study of God's character and the evidence of His Father love that He is not causing the horrific experiences of abuse, sickness, extreme poverty, natural disasters, and the like.

In less extreme cases, God, like a good parent of an adult child, may allow us to experience life and grow up, becoming more mature in our faith. But He never purposefully throws tragedy in our path. God gives us free will to navigate life. Through waiting, trusting, and persevering our faith grows (2 Pet. 1:5-8). We hold onto the promises and we experience God's grace and strength in the midst of our battles (2 Cor.12:9).

At other times, our difficulties can come from our own poor choices. For example, having an accident after choosing to drink and drive, or going to jail after robbing a store are consequences of bad decisions. Some people have had to hit rock bottom to come to their senses, like in the story of the prodigal son. The father didn't follow his son and keep him out of trouble. In his case, the young man had to come face to face with the result of his actions until he saw the state of degradation he had allowed himself to enter. While he was eating pig slop he was forced to face the consequences of his sin, his selfishness, and his stupidity. Only then did he remember his father and determine that he needed to return to his father's house, where he had known love and provision.

God does bring good in the midst of some of life's most painful situations (Rom. 8:28), but that does not mean that what we experienced was part of His plan for our lives. God is so good and so wonderful that He strengthens and carries us through our darkest difficulties; and helps us rebuild our lives.

What about 2 Corinthians 12:7 where Paul says, "I was given a thorn in my flesh"? Does that mean God gave him a sickness? What's a thorn in the flesh? It is not an actual physical problem in your body. It was an expression of the day, just like we use the expression that someone is a "pain in the neck." Notice Paul adds that his problem was "a messenger from Satan." The first occurrence of the thorn in the flesh expression is in Numbers 33:55. God speaks to the Israelites about the unbelieving people that they did not drive out, "those who remain will be like splinters in your eyes and thorns in your sides." Consider Paul's life. He was constantly plagued from town to town by people always coming against his teachings and trying to stop him—religious leaders, local businessmen, governmental officials and, sometimes, even fellow believers. The thorn in his flesh was likely one or more of these people.

Therefore, as we look at the life of Jesus, we are reminded that he came to heal the sick not bring sickness to teach lessons. God is not doing to you what a good earthy father would never conceive of doing. **He has no sinister side.**

The Devil Steals, Kills, and Destroys

Many tragic things that happen in this world and in our lives come from living in a fallen world. Satan is alive and real, but many don't realize this. Adam gave his authority in the world to Satan by disobeying God and essentially worshipping him instead of God. Satan speaks of his own authority to Jesus while they are in the wilderness, *"I will give you the glory of these kingdoms and authority over them,' the devil said, 'because they are mine to give to anyone I please. I will give it all to you if you will worship me'"* (Luke 4:5-7).

Paul and other New Testament writers remind us that the Christian life entails warfare. Paul writes, *"Satan, who is the god of this world, has blinded the minds of those who don't believe"* (2 Cor. 4:4a). Not knowing Satan's tactics, well-meaning Christians feel the need to attribute all of life's experiences, whether good or bad, to God, rather than saying that we don't know why some of the tragedies happen in this fallen world. How sad to attribute evil to God in order to fit our unexplainable life experience.

Unfortunately, if you grow up hearing that God is harsh, does really awful things, and is hard to please, your whole view of God is affected. The perception of God as a cruel taskmaster influences your ability to worship Him, love Him, and know Him intimately, as He desires to be known.

> Once, a young man in a ministry school described his difficult family dynamics. He said, "Well, my mom is like Jesus, but my Dad is like God."

Wow, he had just told me how difficult life had been with his performance-oriented dad. How many people see Jesus as the loving mediator between them and an angry God? Yet, Jesus clearly said, ***"Anyone who has seen me has seen the Father!"*** (John 14:9) (emphasis mine). There are no differences between God and Jesus in how they treat people, how they forgive sins, or how they show unconditional love to all people, from all walks of life.

John described God this way, *"This is the message we heard from Jesus and now declare to you: God is light, and there is no darkness in him at all"* (1 John 1:5). From whom did John hear that message? From Jesus, and He should know. Jesus knew the Father's nature better than anybody has, or ever will. He declared to the world, *"The Father and I are one"* (John 10:30).

The Bible declares that God *is* love (1 John 4:8). Jesus showed the world who the Father really is. Up until that time people had a limited understanding of God, and no real knowledge of Him as a father. The Gospels and other New Testament writings clearly reveal that God is not evil or cruel.

If we want to help a hurting world, we must have the foundational truth of God's goodness solidified in our heart and mind. Many people refuse to believe in God because of the wrong image they have seen portrayed by Christians or because of what they have been taught about Him. ***It is so important that people ministering to others have settled in their hearts, once and for all, that God is 100% good and that He is a good Father.***

Bill Johnson has written an excellent book that explores the goodness of God. *God is Good, He's Better Than You Think* covers the topic in much greater depth than I could ever hope to discuss in one chapter. Johnson writes:

> Believing that God is good is absolutely vital to becoming effective in the ministry of the Gospel. Our endurance in representing Jesus well and consistently is dependent on this one thing. God is absolute goodness. [2]

Besides showing us the goodness of the Father, Jesus exposed the evil nature of the devil. We've looked at Satan's earthly authority but let's consider what Jesus actually says about his mission concerning Satan, "For this purpose, the Son of God was manifested, that He might destroy the works of the devil" (1 John 3:8b, NKJV). Jesus revealed who was behind all the awful things that people had been blaming on God, His Father. Jesus exposed the truth about Satan when He said:

> *"The thief comes only to steal and kill and destroy; I have come that they may have life and have it to the full."* (John 10:10, NIV)

Who brings sickness and terrible disasters? Who delights in orchestrating the inconceivable suffering and pain in the world? Jesus told us, point blank, that it is the devil, or the "thief," as He chose to call him. Jesus comes to bring a life that is full. The devil seeks to destroy and kill. These are some of Jesus' "red letter" words. They are unequivocal.

But What About the Old Testament?

Some people really struggle with understanding some of the records in the Old Testament in light of God's goodness. An important principle of Biblical interpretation is to interpret difficult scriptures in light of the many indisputable ones. We've already discussed how Jesus says that seeing Him, His life, and His character is the same as looking at the Father. Jesus is pure goodness and so is the Father. Yet, people still ignore the absolutely clear scriptures about the goodness of God and focus only on the ones they cannot figure out.

It appears that the people of the Old Testament had only limited knowledge of the devil and his works. There are indications that there was a spiritual war going on even before man was formed in God's image, but the Israelites were unaware of it. Therefore, they attributed everything that happened in the supernatural realm to God. When you worship the devil, as in Baal worship—even to the extent of committing the atrocity of child sacrifice—bad things are going to happen to you. And yet, God got the blame for anything bad that happened.

God won the greatest victory over Satan when Jesus willingly gave His life for us on the cross. The devil had no knowledge or understanding that his killing of Jesus would mean life for us and his own demise (1 Cor. 2:8). Satan's ultimate destruction is only a matter of time.

Jesus came to earth to reveal God as the Father and expose the devil to us. Only then did humanity start to understand what was truly going on in the spiritual realm. Johnson notes, "The nature of His (Jesus) life and purpose is clear and must not be diluted or dismantled by unresolved questions from the Old Covenant. Why did He come? He came to destroy the works of the devil." [3]

Ultimately, we have to study, pray, and decide for ourselves what we believe and determine what beliefs synchronize with the whole Word of God. We must not, however, get too bogged down in minutia. Jesus said that the Pharisees missed who He really was, even though they had delved into the scriptures. *None of our questions, our explanations, or our interpretations of the Old Testament will ever negate the life and words of Jesus Christ.*

A Compassionate God Revealed in the O.T.

The Old Testament book of Jonah is a wonderful story of the unconditional love and patience of God. God's compassion is revealed for one of the wickedest cities on the earth at the time. The people of Nineveh were not even Israelites. Yet God cared about the Ninevites and didn't want them to be destroyed, even though they worshipped heathen gods and were extraordinarily cruel and violent. God told Jonah to go to Nineveh and call the people to repentance. Jonah felt no love or compassion for these people at all. From his perspective, they deserved total destruction. He chose instead to board a ship going to Tarshish, which was in the opposite direction. But Jonah eventually (after a dip in the sea and a remarkable encounter with a large fish) obeyed God. When the king and the people of the city repented and were saved from destruction, Jonah pouted. This prophet of God's rant about the compassion of God is almost comical:

> *Jonah was furious. He lost his temper. He yelled at God, "God! I knew it—when I was back home, I knew this was going to happen! That's why I ran off to Tarshish! I knew you were sheer grace and mercy, not easily angered, rich in love, and ready at the drop of a hat to turn your plans of punishment into a program of forgiveness!"* (Jonah 4:2 MSG)

God responded with a gentle rebuke.

*But Nineveh has more than 120,000 people **living in spiritual darkness**, not to mention all the animals. Shouldn't I feel sorry for such a great city?* (Jonah 4:11, NLT) (emphasis mine)

God's goodness and His redemptive plan are woven throughout the Bible. The coming of Jesus is anticipated in the Old Testament and celebrated in the New. Oral Roberts recorded a message in the 1950s called "The Fourth Man"[4] that is just as impactful today as it was then. He described how Jesus is somehow revealed in every book of the Bible. For example, in the book of Genesis He is "the seed of the woman" and in the book of Ruth, He is shown as "the Kinsman Redeemer."

God loved His people and warned them over and over again about the consequences of turning from Him and worshipping the (Satanic) gods of the nations around them. He warned them just like a mother warns her wayward son against hanging out with the wrong crowd, lest he end up in prison. Sadly, God's people often ignored His warnings and suffered terrible consequences—like capture and enslavement. There is no record of a vengeful, sadistic God reveling maniacally at their pain. God never says I told you so. Instead, when His wayward people wondered if He had forgotten them, scripture reveals His unfailing love:

Yet, Jerusalem says, "The Lord has deserted us; the Lord has forgotten us."
"Never! Can a mother forget her nursing child? Can she feel no love for the child she has borne? But even if that were possible, I would not forget you! See, I have written your name on the palms of my hands." (Isaiah 49:14-16a)

I ask you, does that sound like an angry, judging God? There's so much we just don't understand. But, there's so much that we do. How hard is it to understand Jesus' words to Philip in John 14:9a, "Anyone who has seen me has seen the Father!" Or the author of Hebrews exclaiming in chapter one verse three, "The Son radiates God's own glory and expresses the very character of God." If this is true—that Jesus reveals the character of God—then we can say, without a doubt, that God is a good, good Father!

Reflection and Action

LISTEN

- "Good Good Father" by Housefires

STUDY

- Memorize John 10:10.

- Read 1 John 1:5, John 14:19, 1 John 3:1, the book of Jonah, 2 Corinthians 12:7-10.

JOURNAL

1. What was your relationship with your own father like? Do you see how your relationship with your father affects how you relate to God as a Father and how you see yourself?

2. Do you think God is totally 100% good, or instead, do you think He causes sickness, disasters, or destroys cities in judgment? If so, study the gospels closely. Did Jesus ever cause someone to become sick, or call down fire in judgment on a city that rejected Him? You may also benefit from reading Bill Johnson's book.

3. How will having an understanding of the goodness of God as a loving Father help you as you minister to a world full of hurting people?

CHAPTER 8

Do You Know Who You Are?

"No Longer Slaves" by Jonathan David and Melissa Helser[1]

You Are Accepted and Loved

A group of the leaders' wives from a small church I was attending held a women's meeting. They were eager to share what they had spiritually received from their trip to a church where waves of renewal and revival were being poured out. They spoke about the presence of God coming upon people in unique ways, and asked those who wanted more of God's anointing to come forward. I eagerly stepped forward. Someone prayed a simple prayer over me and said, "More, Lord." For the first time in my life, I slowly fell to the ground, enveloped in a soothing, powerful, weighty feeling of God's presence and love. Tears flowed from my eyes as I heard the Father speaking to my heart about His love for me. The one vivid thing that I will never forget about this time was a mental picture that unfolded as I lay quietly in His presence.

In the vision, people were lined up along a dirt road waiting for Jesus to arrive. I sat there with my legs crossed under me just waiting for my personal time with the Lord. He was going to each person, looking into their eyes, and speaking words of encouragement. Finally, my turn came. He gently cupped my cheeks in His hands. With His beautiful, loving eyes He looked at me with such love and acceptance. Then He gently said, "I didn't ask you to be the perfect mother."

Upon hearing these freeing words, a floodgate of emotional relief erupted from my heart. For about twelve years I had felt guilty, believing that I was not a very good mother. In my mind, I couldn't measure up to what I thought I should be. My house was never that organized. I was not much of a cook. When my children were young, I was extremely sick with hormonal issues and chronic fatigue immune deficiency. Every task seemed like a huge struggle. I had such extreme exhaustion that even making dinner would wear me out. In my children's early years, I'd quickly lose my temper and scream at them, telling them that they were driving me crazy. At least I'd always go back later and apologize and tell them how much I loved them. I'm pretty sure that is partially what saved our relationships.

As time went by, I got better physically through both medicine and prayer. But the feelings of inadequacy remained. I was an involved mother who volunteered at school, read to my boys, sent special notes in their lunch boxes, and told them I loved them. But inwardly I was afraid that I had already ruined their psyche. I could not shake the feeling that I had failed at the one thing in life I wanted the most—to be a good mother. The enemy played on my fears and continued to plant lies in my head. Friends prayed for me to be delivered from "false guilt"; but I was still not free. I could not shake the identity planted in my mind. I truly believed I was a "Bad Mother."

HE WASN'T ASKING ME TO BE THE PERFECT MOTHER OR PERFECT ANYTHING!

That night, seeing *My Jesus*, my sweet Savior, looking into my soul with no anger and no judgment brought total freedom. I felt no shame or fear, just 100 percent unconditional love and forgiveness. He had said the words that I truly needed to hear! He wasn't asking me to be the perfect mother or perfect ANYTHING! This one encounter totally healed my wounded heart and took away my shame. It helped to start me on a journey toward stopping self-condemnation and finding a lasting true identity in Christ.

I've learned that I'm not the only one who feels like they don't measure up. It's easy to compare ourselves with others who seem to be doing much better. God wants us to be free from all comparison. He wants us to know how He sees us. He doesn't judge our performance. He never rejects us; He never disowns us. In Ephesians 1:13b it tells us, *"and when you believed in Christ, He identified you as His own."* The reality is that if we truly surrendered our life to Jesus Christ and asked Him to be our Lord, then we are a totally new person, a new creation (2 Cor. 5:17). Our identity has changed. It doesn't matter what we've done, who our parents are, or what our station in life is. We are now sons and daughters of God, children of "the good, good Father."

Our Father happens to be the King Eternal. Kris Vallotton tells us in his book, *The Supernatural Ways of Royalty*, that we don't have to live in a pauper mentality anymore. We aren't needy people, grabbing for our share, our approval, our fame. We, as Christians, are all part of the royal family. We can live generously. We don't have to perform to be accepted. We are already reigning in this life (Rom. 5:17).[2]

As new creations, we are totally forgiven. Now we can forgive ourselves and others. We have the power to stop living in our old destructive patterns. Romans 6:18 says, *"Now you are free from your slavery to sin, and you have become slaves to righteous living"* (NKJV). We need to hear this. Others do too.

Consider just how life changing this message will be to the people we serve, those struggling in the world. The ones who have been caught in a vicious cycle of hurt and shame long for a new identity and long for freedom.

And consider how important it is for us to be secure and confident in our own identity in Christ. Otherwise, we will overreact in relationships, operate out of a "works" mentality, and not be effective in displaying God's unconditional love. But if we recognize our status as children of God, we can minister with boldness, live in joy, and walk in love.

You Are Identified with Christ

Many Christians understand the concept of being imitators of God and of Jesus Christ. But too few understand *our identification with Christ.* While attending GCSSM, my understanding of the finished work of Jesus Christ deepened and a fire in my heart was rekindled. In class, I heard both Georgian and Winnie Banov address identification with Christ many times as we studied Romans 6, 7, and 8. They loved to remind us of these important scriptural revelations—we were co-crucified, co-buried, co-baptized, co-raised, co-seated in the heavenly realm, and are co-heirs with Christ. The Banovs go into depth about this process of our changed identity in various materials that can be obtained on their website.[3]

The Bible speaks clearly to the truth of our identity with Christ. Romans 6:11 states, *"reckon yourselves to be dead indeed to sin but alive to God in Christ Jesus our Lord"* (NKJV). The word "reckon," which comes from the Greek word *logizomai,* means to "reason to a logical conclusion (decision)."[4]

It is important that you study what the Bible says about identity for yourself. Don't take my (or anyone's) word for it. If you hope to be effective as you minister to others, you have to study the Bible and make it your own. You have to understand for yourself from the revelation of God's Word that you were co-crucified with Christ, and find out in greater dimension what that means.

In his book *Bone of His Bone: Going Beyond the Imitation of Christ,* F. J. Huegel has this to say about Paul's message:

Now what was the central doctrine upon which Paul focused his genius? Was it justification by faith? Many would say that it was. However, a study of Paul's epistles brings one to the conviction that the great apostle's glory was not simply in the fact that Christ had died for him; with that there was always associated another aspect of the cross, namely, the fact that he (Paul) had died in Christ…"I have been crucified with Christ; it is no longer I who live, but Christ lives in me." (Gal.6:14)…For Paul, the Christian life was never to be a mere imitation, but a glorious participation in the Savior's death and resurrection.[5]

Huegel has some other significant things to say regarding the life changing revelation of Christ living within us when he talks about Hudson Taylor, the famous missionary to China. Hudson Taylor had totally surrendered his life to serve God in a far off, and difficult, mission field. Yet apparently, at times, he felt extremely depressed, weak, and insubstantial. This persisted until he got a revelation of his true identity in Christ. Huegel writes:

The apprehension of this principle of our identification with Christ in death and resurrection revolutionized the life and work of a great pioneer in modern missions. And whenever this oneness with the Savior is realized in actual experience, whether it be by the humblest believer or the greatest Christian leader, the same glorious results must follow! Defeat must give place to victory, spiritual poverty and decrepitude to riches of grace and fullness of life. Weakness must give way to power. A burdensome striving to imitate Christ will be changed into a delightful spontaneity in the participation of His divine life. A gnawing sense of insufficiency for Christian life and service will be transformed into a glorious all sufficiency—in a deep union with the all-sufficient Christ![6]

If we are to do the work of ministry with a joyous heart and with lightness of soul, and without a feeling of constant struggle, we must come to understand our oneness with Christ.

You Are a Child of God

The song by Jonathan David and Melissa Helser called "No Longer Slaves," is one of the songs that I highly recommend you add to a worship playlist. Consider these lines: "I'm no longer a slave to fear, I am a child of God."[7] Our understanding of our identity influences how we handle fear. If we don't know who we are in the kingdom of God, then we will be afraid to believe that God could really use us. And yet, there is world of hurting people that are waiting for us to come help them. We have what they need and we don't even know it. We don't believe it could be "us" addressing that need. Fear and broken identity go hand in hand.

If you don't know the authority you hold as a son or daughter of God, the enemy will wreak havoc in your life. You are going to have to face the enemy's attacks, not with just head knowledge, but with a real knowing—from the top of your head to the tip of your toes—of just who you are in Christ. You must believe that you were co-crucified with Christ and were raised to a new life. That you have been adopted into God's family and that you are a child of God.

Trust me, there will come a day, when you are ministering to people, when you get knocked down spiritually, emotionally, and sometimes, even physically. Fear might grip you. The enemy will lie to you, and to others—even putting thoughts in their heads about you. Satan will try to belittle you and make you question who you are. He will try to shame you and bring up your past. Words will flood your mind, "You can't do this. This is too much. Give up. You don't belong in God's family. Look at what you've done."

The Word of God affirms that we are children of God, and knowing His Word will help you resist the lies of the enemy. Romans 8:15-16 says:

> *So you have not received a spirit that makes you fearful slaves.*
> *Instead, you received God's Spirit when he adopted you as his own*

children. Now we call him, "Abba Father." For his Spirit joins with our spirit to affirm that we are God's children.

Knowing you were crucified, buried, and raised to a new life in Christ, accepted and unashamed, will help you believe and become the person God called you to be. Colossians 2:12, and 14-15 says:

> *For you were buried with Christ when you were baptized. And with him you were raised to new life, because you trusted the mighty power of God, who raised Christ from the dead…He canceled the record of the charges against us and took it away by nailing it to his cross. In this way, he disarmed the spiritual rulers and authorities. He shamed them publicly by his victory over them on the cross.*

What right does the enemy have to accuse or shame you? He's the one who got *shamed* when Christ rose from the dead. Unfortunately, He still lies to us about our true identity. On days when his voice is loud and threatening, resist this attack, armed with His Word, and sing out the words to "No Longer Slaves" with the same passion as Melissa Helser. In the song, she really shouts the words *with attitude,* as my inner-city girls might say. Something moves your heart when you hear her sing these words:

> *You rescued me, so I can stand and say*
> *I am a child of God*
> *Yes, I am*
> *I am a child of God*
> *YES I AM*
> *I am a child of God*
> *FULL OF FAITH*
> **I AM A CHILD OF GOD!**[8]
>
> (emphasis mine)

The first time I heard her belting the ending lines of this song, tears actually came to my eyes. What a declaration! What a war cry of victory!

If you are going to successfully minister to others, *prepare your war cry*. With this knowledge, and this belief in your heart of who you really are, you will deal the enemy a decisive blow.

As you embrace your own identity in Christ, as a child of God and as a son or daughter of the King, you will be better equipped to help others embrace a new identity and realize their value. Kris Vallotton encourages us with this message, "May God grant to us the insight to see beyond the outward struggles of people's lives and speak to the treasure that lies within them."[9]

Reflection and Action

LISTEN

- "No Longer Slaves" by Jonathan and Melissa Helser/Bethel Music

STUDY

- Romans 6, 7, and 8, Colossians 2:12, Galatians 6:14, 1 John 3:1-3

JOURNAL

1. Do you struggle with your identity or with performance issues? If so, in what way?

2. What are some things you could do to help yourself grow in embracing the truths about your true identity in Christ (consider teachings, books, women's or men's conferences, worship songs, spiritual mentors).

3. Embracing our true identity can be a struggle for some of us. If it is for you, then consider going for prayer counseling and inner healing sessions.

CHAPTER 9

Are You in Love?

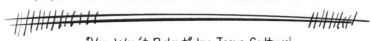

"You Won't Relent" by Jesus Culture[1]

Falling in Love with Jesus

One day during my ninth year at the Center, I went into the guest room in my house that doubled as my prayer room. I was not physically feeling my best and was terribly tired. I lay on the floor listening to worship songs, focusing on how much I loved Jesus. I found myself quietly speaking to Him saying, *Jesus, I KNOW you love me. I know you do. I know you will love me even if I quit running the Center.* As I focused on Him, I got a simple mental picture of Jesus with a single tear trickling down the side of His face.

He looked at me with sad eyes and said, "Yes, I'll love you, but who will love them?"

I didn't expect that. (Of course, He loves them too, but sometimes they need to see Jesus *with skin on.*) So, I determined, once again, not to retire. Not yet. He wanted me to stay and help His kids. I stayed first out of love for Him, and then out of the love He put in my heart for those we were serving.

If you are considering going into ministry, my first question would be:

Are you in love with Jesus?

I mean **in love**, not just, "Yes, I love Jesus." As we become immersed in doing compassion ministry, it is so important that loving intimacy with Jesus Christ is your foundation. God is looking for *"laid-down lovers"*—

which is how Heidi Baker describes passionate followers of Christ. By "laid down lovers," she means people who are willing to lay their lives down because they are so passionately in love with Jesus that they will go and do whatever He asks. Sometimes, that means going across the world to needy orphans. Sometimes, it just might mean stopping and helping someone when it is inconvenient.

We serve out of love. We can't have ulterior motives—like going because we believe the ultimate way to serve God is to be involved in missions. We can't have our identity wrapped up in being a missionary or ministry leader. And we can't serve others just because we feel some kind of condemnation that we are not a good Christian if we don't help "those needy people." We must go because the Lover of our soul loves these people and desires our help reaching out to them in His Name. I know my passionate love for Jesus was the reason that I started Center for Champions—and the reason I stayed.

Without a passionate love for Jesus, we will not last long when the going gets tough. When those cute kids start cussing you out and punching each other, or when you're not seeing any positive changes for the people you are trying to help, it can sometimes feel like you're wasting your time. When various attacks start coming against you, your staff, or your family, it can start to feel overwhelming. You'll reason yourself out of ministering to the needy if the main reason you are there is not for love. Heidi says:

> Just focus on His face. You will only make it to the end if you can focus on His face. Focus on his beautiful face. You can't feed the poor, you can't go to the street, you can't see anything happen unless you see His face. One glance of His eyes, and we have all it takes to lie down. We're not afraid to die.[2]

Ever since I was a little girl, I have known Jesus as my Savior, my King, the Lord Almighty, and My Helper. But I didn't know Jesus intimately, as the Lover of my soul, until I experienced waves of His love wash over me, as I rested in His presence, during certain renewal meetings. It was then that I started to experience His consuming love. God was teaching me in those times how to position myself to get quiet and hear His voice more clearly and intimately.

The Bible says that His sheep hear His voice (John 10:27). All believers can experience knowing Jesus more intimately and hearing His voice more clearly. Jesus calls Himself the Bridegroom. In Revelations 2:4b (NKJV), Jesus says to the church in Ephesus, *"you have left your first love"* Paul describes the church as the body of Christ. He also compares the relationship between Christ and the church to the relationship between a man and his wife. He describes the church as a bride without spot or wrinkle (Eph. 5:25-32).

I started to learn to actively pursue God during those revival years. I already knew that Jesus was the Good Shepherd going to look for the lost sheep. But now, this revelation was different. Here was the Lover longing for His bride, and the bride going out in the streets searching for her Lover (Song of Sol. 3:2). I never understood the Song of Solomon very well until I gained a greater revelation of the meaning of this poetic "song" when I read the Song of Solomon in *The Passion Translation* by Brian Simmons.[3] His translation is an enlightening, and understandable, interpretation of this book of the Bible.

ALL BELIEVERS CAN EXPERIENCE KNOWING JESUS MORE INTIMATELY

I had never realized that Jesus looks at us with such a fiery love. In this poetic text, the Lover represents Jesus. Hear His words:

> *Turn your eyes from me; I can't take it anymore! I can't resist the passion of these eyes that I adore. Overpowered by a glance, my ravished heart-undone. Held captive by your love, I am truly overcome! For your undying devotion to me is the most yielded sacrifice.*
> (Song of Sol. 6:5, TPT)

Jesus loved us so much He was willing to die for us. Are we willing to live our lives completely devoted and in love with Him? Living in love is much more than being an obedient servant. It's obeying and serving out of love. True love is much more than gazing into each other's eyes and singing songs to one another. It requires selfless acts, and being willing to be inconvenienced. It is thinking more of the other person than we do ourselves. It's doing what they ask of us.

Jesus asks us to love. Love is the central theme of Jesus' message to his disciples at the last supper (John 14-17). He speaks of the love of the Father, His love for us, and our love for one another. He says, *"If you love me, keep my commands"* (John 14:15, NIV). Intimacy with Jesus should lead us to the next thing, which is hearing His heart beating for those in need, and obeying if He tells us to go, sharing His love.

Cultivate and Nurture Love

As I am describing what being passionately in love with Jesus looks like, some of you might be saying to yourself that you have never encountered Jesus in such a personal way. You love God and want to be used by Him, but have a hard time "pressing in" to experience an intimate knowing of God. Or maybe you didn't know that such an intimate relationship with God was even possible. God's not asking everyone to relate to Him in the same way. You can encounter God in ways that are unique to you. He's not asking everyone to dance. He's not asking everyone to be outwardly passionately expressive. Not everyone has to feel touched to the point of tears, as I often am. But He does want to touch deep places in *your* heart. He does want to stir a passion in your soul—whatever that looks like in you. Jesus desires to reveal His heart to you personally, so that you can go with a passionate sense of calling into a hurting world.

Sometimes, we need to position ourselves to fall in love. Think about it. What do people do when they fall in love with a future spouse? They pursue each other. They spend every second they can together, and every moment thinking of each other. Similarly, we can make the effort to take time to pursue Jesus. Get quiet in a worshipful way. Remove distractions and rest in his presence. Ask Jesus to reveal His heart, to see His eyes burning with passion for you. Read the Bible, especially those scriptures that pertain to Him. Choose to believe the scripture that says, "*I am my beloved and my beloved is mine*" (Song of Sol. 6:3a, NKJV).

There are several things we can do that can help us grow more intimately in love with Jesus. When we consider our history with Him during difficult times and remember His supernatural strength and grace that helped us through, our love for Jesus grows. When we receive unconditional love and forgiveness instead of punishment when we do something really stupid or wrong, our love grows, perhaps even exponentially. Jesus taught that those who have been forgiven much, love much (Luke 7:47).

There are, however, several things that threatened to snuff out our flame of deep love for Jesus. Life can bring disappointments—perhaps from a seemingly unanswered prayer, or even from the actions of Christians we trusted and to whom we felt close. If we start to blame God for a bad situation, our love for Jesus dies down, and the embers of our passion become a smoldering heap of ashes. For others, our love fades when we get busy and distracted by the mundane—with cell phones, emails, computers, deadlines, and traffic. Or our focus is taken off of Jesus when we are consumed by our responsibilities—family, community, church. Before long we haven't really spent much time with our friend, our lover, our Jesus. Great love affairs can die, you know. We've got to examine our lives from time to time and see if we have put other things before God. Have we really pursued a closer relationship with Jesus lately?

If you are spiritually dry, take time to meet with God. Put yourself where you know that God is moving. Many ministries have equipping and imparting conferences. Make a special effort to go where there is renewal or revival or to a special worship evening. Feel the electricity of the Spirit and the fellowship of so many passionate believers singing love songs to Jesus. If you put yourself next to the burning ones, you will ignite.

Turn Your Eyes Upon Jesus

One of the greatest ways I personally fall more in love with Jesus is when I contemplate the life and ministry of this wonderful Man, as displayed in all of the gospels. I purposely look for and think about the unconditional loving actions and words of Jesus, letting God speak to my heart to reveal aspects of Christ I haven't considered. It's an on-going revelation. Read the gospels for yourself. Renew your mind and heart by finding what the *real* Jesus looks like, putting aside any wrong teachings you've internalized about His character.

Yes, we know Jesus as "the King" when we read Matthew. We find Him as "the Servant" when we read Mark. John shows us in poetic beauty the "Son of God" and Luke reveals "the Son of Man." Get to know Jesus Christ in all of His attributes, but purposely look for *Jesus the Lover*.

See this Man who dearly loved and valued children, taking them up in His arms, and calling us all to be more like them (Luke 18:15-17). Watch Him defend women and elevate their status in a society that devalued them (Matt.26:6-13, Luke 8:1-3). Hear Him say to the woman caught in adultery, *"neither do I condemn you, go and sin no more"* (John 8:11b, NKJV).

See Him speaking to that one hurting, leprous man, who was probably standing a little way off, as the law required, with filthy rags wrapped around diseased fingers and toes. As an outcast, the man hadn't felt the touch of human love for quite some time. The man asked if Jesus would be willing to heal him. Now watch as our Jesus reaches for the man and hugs him in a loving embrace, saying, *"I AM willing!"* (Matt. 8:3b). I venture to say that it was LOVE that healed the man that day.

Contemplate Jesus alone in that garden, on His knees, weeping great pools of tears—blood vessels breaking from the agony of His pain.

The weight of the world and His impending horrendous crucifixion overwhelming His thoughts. Yet, Jesus loved His Father and the world that needed Him so much that He was willing to do what the Father had determined was the only way. *"Abba, Father,' He said, 'everything is possible for you. Take this cup from me. Yet not what I will, but what you will'"* (Mark 14:36, NIV).

See Him on the cross dying for your sins and mine. Jesus willingly endured this humiliation, injustice, and excruciating pain because of His great love for all of the world. He knew this was not the end. Jesus could envision being united someday with His beautiful bride, who is composed of those of us who love Him and who call Him Lord. See Him looking down at the mocking crowd, the Pharisees and the soldiers, yet, praying for them, *"Father forgive them, for they do not know what they are doing"* (Luke 23:34).

See Mary, His mother, standing near the cross, hearing the insults and seeing Him humiliated and tortured. So many questions must have been racing through her mind. He was the Messiah, the one that was prophesied to save her people. She had heard these prophecies even when He was a baby in her womb. The wise men had worshipped Him as a king. She had seen all the miracles Jesus had done. In fact, she had given Him a slight nudge to get His ministry going. Jesus had spoken life and helped so many people. He had done nothing to deserve this punishment. How could this be happening!

But Mary, unlike the other followers that day, was looking at the cross and was seeing her firstborn son being crucified. God had given this amazing woman a prophetic word when Jesus was only a baby. Simeon had said these words, *"He has been sent as a sign from God, but many will oppose him. As a result, the deepest thoughts of many hearts will be revealed. And a sword will pierce your very soul"* (Luke 2:34b-35). That day, those words were all too real. But they did nothing to ease the pain. She doubled over in deep heaves of great sorrow. John was standing by her side.

Now watch as Jesus is dying in agonizing pain and gasps for breath. Yet, still, this loving son remembered His brokenhearted mother. Jesus' bloodshot eyes met the eyes of His beloved mother and those of His friend John. He tried to comfort her with these words, *"Dear woman, here is your son.' And he said to this disciple, 'Here is your mother'"* (John 19:26b-27a). He was seeing to the needs of His widowed mother and providing care for her after His death by entrusting her to someone who believed in His kingdom and would show her great love. Even on the cross, in all His pain, He saw her pain and tried to alleviate it.

This is *My Jesus*, my Friend, my Lover, my faithful amazing wonderful GOD! And He is YOUR Jesus too! Don't you just love Him? Fall in love with this Man. He has already fallen in love with you.

Reflection and Action

LISTEN

- "You Won't Relent" by Jesus Culture
  (cover version of a song written by Misty Edwards)

STUDY

- Song of Solomon 9:6-7 (The Passion Translation), John 19, Luke 18:15-17, Matthew 26:6-13, Luke 8:1-3, John 8: 1-11

JOURNAL

1. What is blocking you from having a more intimate relationship with Jesus Christ?

2. Start reading the four gospels and write down when Jesus shows unconditional love through His actions and words.

3. Write down some of the things that you love about Jesus.

CHAPTER 10

Do You Expect God to Move?

"Here as in Heaven" by Elevation Worship¹

The Father Speaks

He had done it again. He had shouted the "f-word" at another student in his class. He was only six years old, but he could say obscene words as easily as you or I might say, "Stop bugging me." He was one of the cutest, sweetest little guys you could ever meet, always hugging the staff whenever he had a chance. But today that cuteness was not going to help him. Something had to be done. And it was time for him to face some consequences.

The teacher called him up to her desk, and was about to tell him what the consequences would be. But, as he walked up to her desk (she later told us in our staff meeting), she found herself saying, "James, do you know that God is your Father?"

The boy stopped and looked at her, puzzled.

He said, "I don't have a father. He is in prison. And I don't have a mother, either. She died last year."

The teacher tenderly responded that God was his Father, and that He loved James very much. She said, "He is with you always."

The boy looked at her with a surprised, but happy, look on his face. "All the time? Even when I'm sleeping?"

She responded, "Yes, even when you are sleeping."

Then a quiet, and sheepish, look came over his little face as he said, "And I guess He don't like cussing, either, does He?"

God intervened in an amazing way, right in the middle of a disciplinary situation, by bringing a tender conviction. God was revealing the Father's heart to this staff member, so that she could convey His love to a precious, fatherless boy, who needed love and direction. God moved supernaturally because she paused, and looked to see what *the Father might be doing* in that particular situation. John 5:19 states, *"So Jesus explained, 'I tell you the truth, the Son can do nothing by himself. He does only what He sees the Father doing.'"* Too often, we at CFC focused on the program activities, and didn't always tune in to "see." But this time, the staff teacher saw the situation with spiritual eyes.

WE ARE CALLED TO BRING GOD'S KINGDOM TO EARTH.

We are called to bring God's kingdom to earth. As we go about showing love in tangible ways—such as giving out food and clothing, reading to kids, and counseling—we need to recognize opportunities for "God moments." The world has a number of effective social service agencies and NGOs. They all have a place in helping humanity. But, as Christians, we can offer something else—an encounter with God!

In previous chapters, I've shared a few God encounters and some of the many supernatural ways that God supplied our finances. I want to relate to you some additional testimonies of God moving in our small program. Nothing I present is a formula for how God works. These testimonies are to build your faith and encourage you to *expect God to move in supernatural ways,* as you pray and partner with Him!

Healing Power Encounters

One of the CFC past program directors, Richie, had a burning desire to see God reveal Himself as the Healer. (He has even written a user-friendly book called, *Moving Mountains: How to See the Sick Healed and the Captives Set Free*.)

Richie taught about healing in our chapel times and even taught the children how to pray for each other. Once, they prayed for a ten-year-old boy, and immediately he said his hearing in one ear was healed. Later, we contacted his mother to check on him. Sure enough, he had been partially deaf in that one ear and now he could hear!

Another time at chapel, Richie asked if anyone needed healing. A college student from Messiah College, who volunteered at the Center, showed everyone her broken arm that was in a cast. The kids surrounded her, laid hands on her, and prayed for her arm to be totally healed. The next day she felt no pain, and she really believed it was healed. She went to the doctor and asked him to take off the cast. He was hesitant because the cast had been on for less than a week. So, he took another x-ray. To his surprise, her broken arm was totally healed!

One of the most amazing testimonies of healing was when a teenage boy described a supernatural encounter that brought healing. The staff and youth were praying for healing for a few of the children who were not feeling well that day. Most responded that they felt better after the prayer. However, one teenager, who had hurt his wrist in sports practice, said his wrist didn't feel any better. Richie, who had learned to be tenacious about healing, told him that he would pray for him again later after he completed some work that needed to be done.

Richie had to do a task on the computer in the main office, so he asked this boy to sit on the sofa while he typed. But while he was working, the boy fell asleep on the office sofa. About ten minutes later, he got up and stood by the computer. He looked at Richie with tears streaming down his face and told him that Jesus had appeared to him in his dream and touched his wrist. Upon waking, his pain was completely gone. He was so amazed that Jesus had healed him. And we were amazed, hearing about his encounter with Jesus!

Once, I took the eight-year-olds to walk the city streets. We encountered a local police woman and the children asked if she'd like them to pray for her. She said that she'd like that, so they prayed for God's protection over her life. Then, they prayed for a man's leg that was in a brace. He was supposed to have the brace on for several more weeks. When I saw him a week later on the street, he yelled out, "Tell those kids my doctor said my leg got so much better, so fast."

The Divine Mechanic

The last year that I worked for the Center we had gotten off to a delayed start by several weeks. Four months earlier, the board had even been discussing whether to close the Center, but God had made a way for us to continue. Yet, as it became time to start the new school year, one thing after the other kept us from starting as planned. Finally, it was the first day for the kids to attend.

While we were in a staff meeting, I got a call from our bus driver. She told me that she couldn't get the bus to start. She had already picked up a few of the kids from their schools, but still needed to get about 30 more. I told her we would pray, and then call her back.

Frankly, this was another one of those "this-is-the-last-straw" kind of days, and we were quite tired of the enemy's opposition to the start of the program. Something welled up inside the hearts of the staff. There are times when you pray and then there are times when you are not really praying, but instead you are actually declaring the promises of God. This was one of those declaring times. (We remembered the story where an axe head fell in water, and Elisha was able to miraculously get that metal axe head to float through an act of faith.) With the Word of God in our thoughts, we declared that nothing is impossible with God. We took authority in the name of Jesus over the situation. We declared that this bus was going to run, and that those kids were going to arrive at the Center that day. I called the bus driver back and asked her to try to start the bus again.

She said, "Miss Denise, I already tried four times!"

I said something about the fact that we had prayed, and asked her to just try it one more time. She reluctantly agreed to try it. *It started right up.* I asked her if she felt it was working okay and safe to drive. She said she felt like it was. She got all the kids from the schools and to the Center. Then, I followed her to our mechanic to make sure there was nothing seriously wrong. She drove the bus through the city streets, through many stop lights, finally pulling into the shop. By then, the brakes were feeling soft, so we asked if the mechanic could just take a look at them. He got up and poured brake fluid in, and it poured right out on the ground under the bus. Perplexed, he asked how we got the bus to his shop. We told him that she had just driven it over. He looked at us like we were crazy, and told us that the bus had no working brakes, at all.

We just started laughing out loud. Now, he knew we were crazy. Most people would be upset knowing they were going to have to pay for an entire bus brake system. But I was so excited! I started telling the mechanic how God had miraculously made a way for the kids to get to the Center that day. I even started telling him the Bible story about Elisha and the axe. He just sort of half smiled at me as if he was thinking, *"OK, lady, I get it."* I wanted to give God the praise for the victory of no more delays in the start of our program. (Of course, we would not have driven the bus with the kids in it, if we had known the brakes were bad—just in case some of you were wondering!)

A Broken Phone Works and Violence Averted

Once, I believe a man's life was saved from violence, as God intervened through one of our staff members. Our first program director, Eric, had a father's heart for both the youth in our after-school program and the tough young adult men in the neighborhood. He ran a successful basketball program called "Knight Hoops" that ran from 10 p.m. to midnight. One afternoon, he was planning to pick up some of the guys for the game, but his phone had not been working all day. He needed to get in contact with one young man, in particular, to tell him he'd be by to pick him up. He decided to give it one more try. This time, surprisingly, his phone finally worked.

The young man told Eric that he had just been robbed by someone he knew. He said that he was planning to go find the guy and shoot him. Eric, calm as usual, didn't try to talk him out of it, but wisely just convinced him to come to the basketball game. Before the games, the players and coordinators always had a "team talk." The talk that day most likely saved both his and the other guy's lives, because during the meeting that night, all the players convinced him to forget it, and not mess with the robber. So, what was supernatural in this incident? Of course, God's still voice of wisdom to Eric, but also the fact that even though his phone had not been working all day, this one call went through. Yep, our God is bigger than the devil's plans (and technology!).

OUR GOD IS BIGGER THAN THE DEVIL'S PLANS (AND TECHNOLOGY)!

Emotional Healing in His Presence

For many years, we took several of our inner-city mothers to Life Center's women's retreat. They loved the worship, the speakers, and the fellowship with other women. One Friday night, however, although the service was good, the topic discussed was not that relatable to our moms. That night, some of us prayed that the next morning there might be something shared that would really touch their hearts. Morning came, and the speaker, Carol Arnot, seemed to veer off her topic, and suddenly started telling us about letters she had received from people in prison. She recounted some of their pain from abusive fathers and from others in their lives. I looked down the line of five CFC mothers seated next to us. All of them had tears streaming down their faces.

God had orchestrated this moment for these ladies. Then, instead of calling people up for prayer, Carol told us to move all the chairs to the sides of the room. Everyone was asked to just lie on the floor, while worship music played. She prayed that the Father would speak to our hearts. It was clear that God was supernaturally touching those women that day, bringing healing to their hearts.

There was one mother in particular who had been guarded and hardened prior to this encounter. After that weekend, she wanted to meet me for lunch. She opened up for the first time, and talked about some of the abuse and other difficult things that had happened in her life. The encounter she had with the Father at the retreat had started to peel away some of the walls she had put up, and softened her heart to be able to receive additional healing.

Anointed Dance and Creative Arts

One cold, early Easter morning at a sunrise service, we were all freezing outside on the city street. During the service, our dance team from the Center did an expressive dance to Nicole Mullen's song, "I Know My Redeemer Lives." The joy and the grace that emulated from these young girls, whom we knew did not have easy lives, was incredibly moving. Our hearts were warmed and nobody seemed to notice the cold anymore. I looked over, and there was my practical engineer husband with tears in his eyes. I always say when people tell me that they don't really "feel" the presence of the Holy Spirit, that *tears count.* That wasn't the first or last dance performance where members in the audience shed tears. It happened so many times. God's presence would anoint the dancers, and touch the audience, as they worshipped Him in this way.

Prophetic Ministry

There was a mother who wanted to talk with me about her thoughts on whether or not to accept Jesus as Lord and become a Christian. She said she didn't want to be like those people who said they were Christians, but didn't act like it. So, I just loved her where she was, and invited her to come to a weekend women's retreat that many of us were attending.

The first night of the retreat, someone who had never even met her slipped a piece of paper into her hand. The mom was so encouraged and amazed as she read prophetic words specifically for her. She asked me how this woman, whom she'd never met, could know so much about her. I explained a little about prophetic words and how this was God's way of speaking to her heart. Early the next morning of the retreat, this mom told me that she was now ready to become a Christian. We prayed, right then and there, with pajamas on and rollers in our hair.

Praying prophetically for people is one of the greatest tools for touching people's hearts. I wish we had known more about it in the beginning years of CFC. In the past few years, Linda, our family counselor, and Steve, a compassionate minister, with training in inner healing, have prophetically prayed as they counseled with some of the mothers, fathers, and even children in the program. Lovingly sharing words that they hear the Father saying specifically for each person has brought freedom in many areas to those they have counseled.

When praying prophetically, the goal is to hear and impart a message from the Father's heart. It is not so much about knowing future events or some special fact about the person. Shawn Bolz, a young man incredibly gifted in the prophetic, wrote this in his recent book:

The prophetic is one of the greatest tools of love we have…through it we see a very real glimpse of God's heart and get to treat people exactly the way God intended them to be treated from the beginning.[2]

Compassion ministry leadership and other ministry workers can benefit so much from learning to operate in the prophetic. The world needs to experience God, not just hear a teaching about Him. A prophetic word that speaks directly to someone from the Father's heart is a powerful tool in ministering to others.

The Bible says in 1 Corinthians 14:1, *"Let love be your highest goal! But you should also desire the special abilities the Spirit gives—especially the ability to prophesy."* You don't have to be a prophet to prophetically pray for people or to relay messages from the Father's heart.

Expect God to Move

I am always amazed at stories of miraculous experiences by missionaries in Africa, or God appearing in dreams to people in the Middle East. I can easily wonder, *Why is God always moving somewhere else?* But, as I reflect back, some amazing things happened right here in our town with just a bunch of "little ole me's" regularly ministering to about 50 kids and 25 parents. If God can do it for us, He can do it in your ministry, too! I pray that these stories of how God moved in amazing ways will encourage you to *expect* God to partner with you as you minister to others.

I am confident we would have seen even more of God's supernatural involvement if we had just slowed down and waited on Him. We did see miracles and lives changed. However, when I look back over sixteen years, I now see that sometimes those special days were too few and far between. Too often, we let the urgency of the moment, and the activities we planned for the week, take priority. Take my advice—***Make room for God to move in your ministry.***

God wants to be involved in our lives and ministries in powerful ways, but sometimes He waits for us to ask. Pray, and ask God to move in your ministry. Of course, He's watching over you, directing your steps, bringing sovereign divine appointments, and protecting you in ways that you may never know. But there's so much more that He will do supernaturally, through us, if we ask and position ourselves to see what the Father is doing. Expect to see more of God's miraculous involvement as you minister to others, and your faith might be wondrously rewarded.

Reflection and Action

LISTEN

- "Here as in Heaven" by Elevation Worship

STUDY

- John 14:12-14, 2 Kings 6:1-6, 1 Corinthians 14:1, Hebrews 11:1-12, James 5:13-18

JOURNAL

1. Think of several occasions when you saw God intervene supernaturally. Was there a particular hunger for or prayer for His intervention at that time? Or were you surprised by how He moved?

2. Have you ever been given a prophetic word? How did it make you feel? Did it influence your life or your perspective in some way?

3. Why do you think we don't see as many miraculous occurrences here in America as in third world countries?

SECTION IV

Persevering Through Challenges

CHAPTER 11

Running in Sync with the Team

"How He Loves" by John Mark McMillan[1]

Relationships and Resolving Interpersonal Conflicts

Have you ever had a wonderful quiet time with God while listening to a passionate worship song? Afterwards, you come out of your prayer closet convinced that it is going to be a great day! You name the day, "Bliss." But then you turn on your computer and find an e-mail from a co-worker telling you how you offended them or someone else. Or, perhaps someone calls up to complain about a person on your team or a person your ministry was trying to help. Suddenly, you are no longer feeling blissful. You start to feel somewhat perturbed.

Later, maybe you get a text asking about the flyers your teammate was supposed to complete. You text that person to find out what happened, and they reply that they forgot. (This is not the first time.) Now you have to do something that you felt the other person could have easily taken off your already-too-full plate. Others had suggested you delegate more, so you did. But now you start to think that you shouldn't have even bothered.

Or maybe you had a difficult decision to make. You prayed and asked God for wisdom. You felt sure you had an answer. There was peace. But then as you share your decision in the staff meeting, someone you really respect questions your decision in front of the others and will not let it go. You leave the staff meeting feeling frustrated, embarrassed, and starting to doubt yourself. Sometimes, real life just feels so vexing.

It is times like these when you want to go back into that "prayer" room, bedroom, or car—wherever you and God talk—and say these words, "Father I love you very much...but *your people* are driving me crazy. Why do I have to deal with all of these frustrating people? What are you doing to me?" Moses had people problems, too. He once complained to God in a rather dramatic way, *"Did I conceive all these people?"* (Num. 11:12a NKJV).

When you're starting up a ministry you probably aren't thinking about how well your team will work together relationally. I know that it never crossed my mind. I just sought out others who shared the same vision for helping inner-city children. It quickly became clear how differently we each approached this type of ministry. I gradually came to realize that the more aware I was of potential pitfalls in the relationships among our team members, the better we could address concerns, forgive weaknesses, and find common ground while serving together in love.

I hope my being so honest about interpersonal issues that one might face while serving in ministry does not scare you away from stepping out and getting involved. I have attended several ministry schools and conferences over the past twenty years. These meetings taught me so many wonderful things about God's love, our identity in Christ, and our call to pray for healing with faith and action. But I remember one session that I found particularly helpful to my life because interpersonal conflict in ministry was actually discussed.

The session was taught by a woman named Lesley-Anne Leighton. She taught a ministry school called _Holy Given International School of Missions_ at Life Center in 2006. Her words in that particular session gave me hope when I saw that others had struggled as we had and that the problems we were facing were normal. So, don't be surprised if relationship struggles happen in Christian ministry. In fact, prepare to navigate interpersonal relationship dynamics, and hopefully you will handle problems in a better manner than I did.

It is encouraging to know that some of the co-workers with whom I often butted heads and whose personalities were so different from mine are now people that I extremely admire. I refer others to them for help. And I consider some of them my closest and dearest friends. Proverbs 27:17 (NIV) declares, *"As iron sharpens iron, so one person sharpens another."* Don't become disillusioned by relationship conflicts. Choose to love your teammates, who are your comrades in battle, as you minister to the needy. Practice and consider the truths found in 1 Peter 4:8, *"Most important of all, continue to show deep love for each other, for love covers a multitude of sins."* Determine to see your team members—and those you serve—as Christ sees them. The world needs to see believers who are united in purpose and in heart, who actually love each other.

Charles Stock has some words of wisdom about relationships, "Here are a few key principles that will keep you healthy in the midst of the ambitions and pressures of leadership: Love is the greatest. Whatever you do, don't sacrifice love for the sake of "winning" a dispute, gaining advantage, or promoting your own fame."[2]

Charles goes on to remind us how much we really need each other to accomplish our mission. He states, "The heaven-sent projects and visions that burn in your heart can only be appropriately expressed in relational integrity, true love shining within your own inner and outer communication. *The interaction within your team is the greenhouse for changing the world!*"[3] (emphasis mine). I'd say this makes working for good relationships and pursuing love among the team quite worth the effort.

The Enemy Seeks to Divide

I wish I had known that attacking the unity of believers who are serving together is one of Satan's biggest strategies. He hates that we want to bring love where there is hate, hope and freedom where there is captivity, and light where there is darkness. When we are prepared and know his games, we are able to overcome his schemes. If I had known how intently

Satan tries to ruin relationships in the beginning stages of our ministry, I would have been on the lookout sooner. I would have handled situations differently, and shown more grace. Once we finally got this revelation, we were usually able to reconcile issues, if all involved were willing to do so, before they got out of hand.

"And if a house is divided against itself, that house cannot stand" (Mark 3:25 NKJV). Satan has been trying to divide ministries for centuries. In Acts 15:35-41, we read that Paul and Barnabas parted ways after their first long mission trip. They had a disagreement about taking along John Mark (Barnabas' nephew) on the next mission trip because he had left them while on the last one. Paul did not want John Mark to come along while Barnabas did. There are a few interesting Bible study commentaries online that actually show how some positive results came out of this situation. For example, two mission teams went out to two different places and more people were reached with the message of Christ. These commentaries also point out that Paul changed his mind about Mark years later, even describing him as helpful (2 Tim. 4:11).[4]

One time, while in a ministry school, I was assigned to read a five-hundred-page book about missions in the last one hundred years. I was so excited when we got this assignment. But by page four hundred, I became so sad and discouraged after reading how many ministries fell apart due to relationship issues that I flung the book across the floor.

In one of her sessions at my church, Lesley Anne Leighton told a story[5] about herself and one of her interns that illustrates how steadily Satan works to divide those in ministry together. Lesley really appreciated having this young woman's assistance in helping to carry her vision and some of the work load. They were getting along fine, no arguments, and nothing separating them.

But one night, as she slept, the intern had dreams about Lesley-Anne. In the dreams, there were many derogatory things bombarding her thoughts about this leader. The things were not true but were a vivid part of her dreams. When she awoke, she was convinced that there was some truth in her dream and began to speak and act negatively towards Lesley Anne. Eventually they talked about what was bothering the intern. During their discussion Lesley Anne was able to correct the lies and half-truths brought up in that dream. The intern began to realize that those thoughts were not even her subconscious thoughts *but were thoughts planted in her mind by the enemy.* Fortunately, they talked and reconciled, and were then alert to Satan's tactics.

I was stunned. Finally, I had others confirming what I had come to believe about the enemy's role in miscommunication. And this was from a respected leader, who was saying that the enemy actually puts thoughts against one another in our minds.

Another leader, Pastor Reinhard Hirtler, wrote a book called *The Power to Forgive, How to Overcome Unforgiveness and Bitterness.* The book shows why and how to forgive people step-by-step. Hirtler describes how one person may be saying something, but the other person hears it completely differently. I'm not talking about normal miscommunication, when people are not listening to each other very well. I am talking about mixed up words, and words planted that were not even said. The consequences are alarming and it can take great love and a lot of talking it out to gain clarification in order to correct the miscommunication. Hirtler gives a name to this demonic influence that mixes up communication. He calls it an "apple-banana demon."

Hirtler writes, "Most Christians I talk to agree that they have experienced the activities of this apple-banana demon. The demon has a specific purpose—to twist words ... Of course, there is not a literal demon called the apple-banana demon, but this is how I classify him because it helps me understand what is going on at times."[6] This demon affecting communication is sometimes responsible for serious offenses between people. It is so important to talk things out, check out what is truth, and determine to listen to what the other person is saying.

Learning to Work Together

While Satan and his forces seek to divide, we ourselves also cause much conflict in our relationships. It is our personal frailties, our ambitions, our personality types, our emotional issues, and our inner wounds that can play a big part in how we relate to, and even hurt, one another. It's important that we express clearly what we mean and learn to listen well. Materials that deal with communication and inner healing are listed at the end of this book in the recommended resources. Some resources address how to gain better communication skills which include speaking with *"I Messages"* and *"Actively Listening."*

To minister effectively we must address areas where we have personal emotional wounds. Simply by living life in this world we will receive wounds from others. Some people have experienced serious abuse and neglect. Often, those who have been wounded, wound others. Sometimes, however, those who have been seriously wounded are the most compassionate toward others. These individuals may decide to get involved in ministry and have much to offer, especially in the area of empathy. However, at the same time, these individuals need to do all they can to find personal inner healing so that they don't end up hurting those they seek to help.

TO MINISTER EFFECTIVELY WE MUST ADDRESS AREAS WHERE WE HAVE PERSONAL EMOTIONAL WOUNDS

While working together with other people in ministry, it is very important to practice what Jesus told us to do in situations when we offend each other. In Matthew 18:15-17 it says to *first talk between just the two of you.* Don't go to someone else to complain about the leader or the other staff person. Then, if you do not understand each other, bring along another person or two to mediate. I have seen some positive results with mediation. If things are still not worked out, Matthew speaks of bringing the person or issue to the church. In a ministry, I'd say, you'd bring it to the board. If nothing can be resolved, then you may have to forgive each other and just agree to disagree. In some cases, you may need to part ways in a spirit of respect and goodwill. It's not the end of your ministry. It's not some big failure. It's just that two people had different visions, different ways of doing things, and they just couldn't work together effectively.

Expectations and Giving Grace

The expectations we bring to our ministry are often the source of the frustrations between team members. People can't read our minds. Sometimes, we don't effectively verbalize what is needed. Sometimes we are expecting too much, too fast. Sometimes, maybe we need to lower our expectations and give people some space, and some grace. I know we want to operate with excellence. But, you know what, dare I say it, Jesus never asked us to be excellent. He just asks us to be *faithful*.

Ministry can be hard, and sometimes messy. We are serving people with serious needs and oftentimes with dysfunctional lives. Things often don't go as planned. Perhaps, people on the team should have handled a situation in a different way. Or maybe we are the ones who dropped the ball, and then we beat ourselves up emotionally about our mistakes. Don't do it. Remember, God isn't asking you to be *perfect*, and you shouldn't expect perfection of yourself or others.

We may think that something should be done a particular way. Guess what I learned? God can use many ways to accomplish the same thing. We may think someone should have known something that they didn't know. If you are working with young adults, it helps to remember how you were when you were in your twenties. It took me a while to learn these things, to lessen my expectations, to delegate more, and to be more grateful. If you are leading a ministry and depending on a team, which will most likely include part-time staff and/or volunteers, you may need to modify your expectations. Learn to truly appreciate the many good things that *are* getting done. Weigh that against what is not so "up-to-par." Have patience. Train and teach where there is lack of understanding. But do it all with GRACE, GRACE, GRACE. Heidi Baker shares in her book, *Reckless Devotion*:

> Here's what I've realized: We are supposed to work together and help each other. We are not all meant to be capable of doing everything. We are gifted to do some things, while others are completely beyond us. That's okay. That's how God made us. He made us to need each other—and to need Him.[7]

Jesus Showed Grace to his Fellow Companions

John 1:17b (NKJV) reads, *"grace and truth came through Jesus Christ."* Of course, we know of His amazing saving grace for our salvation, but I want to list a few ways that Jesus *showed grace* to His fellow "compassion ministry" workers. It helped me, so much, when I considered how Jesus treated and reacted to some of the things His disciples said or did. In a number of situations, they didn't act or respond very well. Honestly, sometimes these grown men acted like adolescent boys. So, in dealing with our own relationship problems in ministry, let's put things in perspective. ***How did Jesus lead?***

Do you have a situation where those you depend on in leadership positions frustrate you with their attitudes and actions? Two of Jesus' disciples—grown men—who had been some of His closest companions, had their mother come to Jesus and ask Him to give her sons special positions in His kingdom. The other disciples got mad when they heard about it. But Jesus did not condemn the two disciples and instead used that as a time to teach more truth about His kingdom (Matt. 20:20-28).

The disciples' arguments did not end with this incident. On the most somber and serious night that Jesus would ever have with his disciples, they were still arguing about who was the greatest. *Really?* But, Jesus didn't tell them to leave. Instead, He picked up a wash basin, and gave them a lesson in humility and service that they would never forget.

Have you ever asked some of your team to cover for you during a challenging time, only to find they didn't follow through? Consider Jesus in the garden of Gethsemane. He was in deep agony. He needed that time alone with the Father. All He asked was that His disciples would watch and pray. But instead of looking past their own concerns and doing what Jesus asked and covering Him in prayer, they fell asleep. Jesus comes to Peter and asks in astonishment, *"couldn't you watch with me, even one hour?"* (Matt. 26:40, NKJV). You can almost hear the disappointment in His statement. But, He didn't tell them to go home. He didn't scream at them, even in His state of agony. Instead, Jesus gives them grace by acknowledging that, *"The spirit is willing but the flesh is weak"* (Matt. 26:41).

Some have felt betrayed by others who have left their ministry? Did that ever happen to you? Perhaps, someone left and proceeded to speak against your leadership and the ministry. Think how much more cruelly Jesus was betrayed by Judas and others. But while Jesus was on that cross, He said, *"Father forgive them for they don't know what they are doing"* (Luke 23:34). He forgave them all—the soldiers, the Pharisees, the crowds who cried "crucify him," the disciples who ran away, and even Judas.

Perhaps you encountered a situation where your right-hand staff person was hesitant to back you up in a meeting? It can feel pretty awful. Maybe no one defended you, while unjust accusations were being made against your leadership. Well, Peter, who ministered with Jesus for three years, when faced with the fear of being arrested himself, completely denied association with Jesus. The Bible says that Jesus turned and looked at him at that moment. Don't think Jesus didn't feel the sting of rejection. He had become human like you and I. But after Jesus was resurrected He completely forgave Peter, and even established him as a prominent leader.

Jesus had a team that included so many different personalities, including Peter and John. At times, they let Him down. Some days, they had arguments among themselves. But Jesus believed in giving people the benefit of the doubt and a second chance. He believed in giving people grace. Can we do any less!

Reflection and Action

LISTEN

- "How He Loves" by John Mark McMillian

STUDY

- 1 Peter 3:8-12, Philippians 2:1-12 and 14-16, Matthew 18:15-17, Ephesians 4:1-6 and 21-32

- Read Bob Deffinbaugh's online study about the split between Paul and Barnabas.

- Read "When Division Becomes Multiplication."
  Found here: bible.org/seriespage/24-when-division-becomes-multiplication-acts-153-1610

JOURNAL

1. Have you ever been in a situation where you were saying one thing and the other person heard something completely different? How did it get resolved?

2. Do you know your personality type? How might your personality type affect your interaction with others? Consider looking into some personality tests. Ask friends for feedback. Knowing yourself is infinitely helpful when trying to relate to others well.

3. Do you remember a time when someone offered you grace and the benefit of the doubt when you really messed up? Felt good, didn't it? Is there a situation in your life where you could extend the same grace?

CHAPTER 12

Wounded People Wound People

"Song of Solomon" by Martin Smith[1]

Wounded Warriors

As you decide to step out to address the concerns and needs of those God calls you to help, it's quite likely, actually almost guaranteed, that you will be wounded at some point. But that's no reason to avoid the battle. God is looking for unlikely heroes to go into spiritual battlefields to set the captives free. This means you will often be under attack. Some of the enemy's bullets will land around you and some will be a direct hit. But the reward of going to help those in need will far outweigh the battle scars. I remember, all too well, one particular time when I received a direct hit.

Preparations for God Encounters

I lugged my three-foot-tall electric water fountain down to the room at the end of the hallway where we were preparing for the parent's dinner that night. I was in the process of setting the atmosphere in this room that we had set aside for spiritual "soaking," complete with candles and Dove chocolates in baskets by the door. I pressed play on the *Father's Love Letters* CD.[2] As I heard the words flow from that recording—scripture after scripture of the Father's love—my heart swelled. *Aww,* I thought. *Yes, this will be so good for these ladies to hear.*

I wanted these single mothers to have an experience with the Father's heart that night, not just hear a teaching. I wanted God, the Heavenly Father, to speak to their deepest parts, showing them how much He loved them, as He had done so many times for me. Downstairs, loyal volunteers decorated each table with pretty flowers, favors, and tea candles. My husband was cooking the steaks, and the kitchen was bustling with preparations for our annual Mother's Day evening event.

Several women from our church arrived to volunteer and serve the CFC moms. One of the more impactful ways they served was by going over the meaning of a Bible verse that each mom would randomly select from a basket. After talking about the verse, they would pray with each mother about any concerns she had weighing on her heart, and provide prophetic words of encouragement. Among all of the many special things that we did at those Mother's Day dinners year-after-year, the individual prayer time was always the favorite of the moms.

Years before, when God broke my heart about what was happening in the inner city, He made it clear that Center for Champions should be a program for the parents as well as the kids. He had heard their cries for their children, and saw the pain they had endured. These women were survivors. Now, they were determined that their children would have "better," if they could possibly do something about it. We knew God wanted to reach the hearts of these moms and let them know how much He loved them.

Cries of a Wounded Soul

The moms arrived, and their children, who had already eaten, went to the parking lot area to play. The evening progressed beautifully. The Center for Champions girls' dance team performed in the theater for the mothers, and then joined their friends to play games. As the evening was coming to an end, I was sitting in the prayer room, feeling so thankful that everything had gone as planned. Tissues were being passed around to wipe the tears streaming down many of the mothers' cheeks. The women were experiencing love in action. There was a strong sense of God's Presence.

But, suddenly, one of the kids burst into the room, yelling, "Miss Denise, come quickly, they're fighting!"

I jumped up and dashed out of the room. The mothers got up to see what was going on. They quickly collected their things and walked out into the lobby of the church, preparing to get on our bus. Staff members briefed me about a fight that had broken out. One of the middle school girls had hit another girl, and then a few of their cousins had gotten involved. By the time I got to the lobby, our program director had broken up the fight and had the situation under control.

I was determined not to talk about the issue with the parents that night, or even to make a decision about any disciplinary action. But the mother of the girl who started the fight kept badgering me about what I was going to do.

I said, "We aren't going to talk about it right now. Everyone get on the bus."

But she would not let up. She was an intimidating woman, who towered over me. She'd recently come to the area from Harlem in NYC. I knew she had a pretty hard life, and that her life experiences had taught her to distrust most people. She had already made it clear that she assumed I didn't like her three daughters who were in the program. That was definitely not the truth, but I couldn't get her to believe this, especially since, in the past, it had become necessary to send her daughters home occasionally because of behavioral issues.

She started yelling that it was a particular girl who had started the fight. I had known this girl for a long time. She'd never been a fighter, or a problem in our program. (Plus, the staff had already told me what had happened and she was definitely not to blame.)

I made a big mistake and responded to the mother saying, "I doubt it was that girl's fault."

My exasperated words were all that this angry mother needed to confirm her raging accusations. "F—k you, Miss Denise," she screamed loudly as everyone watched—the kids, the staff, the parents, and my friends from the church.

I gasped, then yelled, "Everybody, get on the bus. Now!" Then I rushed to the ladies' bathroom.

A friend happened to be in the lobby, so she came in after me. I bent over the sink clutching my side. It felt like I had been literally stabbed. Honestly, it did. Deep sobs poured out. I just couldn't believe this, and thought to myself, *After all I have done for these women. This is how they treat me.*

I COULD FEEL MYSELF HARDENING TOWARD THE PEOPLE GOD CALLED ME TO CARE ABOUT

I started to be inwardly offended, and said to my friend, "I can't do this anymore. I just can't do it."

Every ounce of energy was drained from my soul. I was numb. One more piece of my heart had been ripped out, and I could feel myself hardening toward the people God had called me to care about. Of course, it wasn't all the moms. All the other mothers had been appreciative of the evening. It was just this one mom, but in my distress, it seemed as if they were all against me.

Need for Healthy Boundaries

The problem in this scenario was not that particular woman. There were a number of factors that made this situation unbearably painful to me. First, I had forgotten the cardinal rule of social work, which should be a rule for ministry work also: you must have emotional boundaries when working with wounded people. In my love and concern to make the evening unforgettable for the moms, I had completely let my guard down. This woman had had a horrendous life growing up. Her self-esteem was extremely low. She was ashamed, not wanting to believe or admit that it was her child that had caused the problem. She took that anger and embarrassment and put it on me. Perhaps her words hadn't even contained the hateful venom that I felt. She was used to being around people who talked that way to each other all the time.

However, I grew up in the 60s in a rural small town, in a family where the "f" word was as bad as the "n" word—neither was ever to be uttered from one's mouth. In those days it was the meanest, nastiest thing you could say to anyone. Her saying it to me, in front of everybody, hurt me deeply. But it shouldn't have hurt *that deeply*.

I realized that night that I had to set up more boundaries. I had to turn over some of the duties of working with the parents to another staff member, because, as the executive director, I was always going to be viewed as the authority person. Some of the other moms, who had experienced past abuses from authority figures at various times, had also responded to me with distrust and anger. They could not really believe that I had their children's best interest in mind. They had "bitter-root" judgments or expectations from experiences in their past that they illogically transferred to whatever situation was in front of them. I needed to stop the attacks by not being one of the main people with whom they were engaging.

When working with people who have had a difficult past, it is important to remember that they often filter what is going on in the present through the things that happened in their past. If someone has experienced very little love, acceptance, and protection from their parent(s) or other authority figures, and if they continued to be beaten down by others, the results are fear and low self-esteem. They feel that nobody can be trusted. Some become combative, especially toward people in positions of authority. I should have remembered all this, especially considering my education and experience in social work.

This woman and I eventually reconciled and forgave each other. But I also determined it was best for me not to be the one ministering to her needs. I decided that another staff person should become our family coordinator and be the person who worked most directly with the parents. I loved the mothers, hugged and prayed for them, and planned programs for them. But from then on, I didn't spend as much time with the mothers in the program.

The staff member we chose to become our family coordinator was a loving person, a good listener, gifted in counseling, with skills for doing "inner healing," and someone the mothers related to very well. You'll need to look at your team, and see who has the best gifting to work directly with the people you are trying to help. Some work great with children. Some work well with adults. Some are good program leaders. Love the people God called you to love. But, also, love your team of mission workers, and wisely put in place reasonable boundaries.

Another reason I was so affected by this mother's harsh words was my own compassion fatigue. I needed to do more to take care of myself. I wasn't carving out enough quiet time to be with God, spending time in nature and doing relaxing hobbies, or delegating enough responsibilities to other staff. We had a small staff and all of us probably carried more responsibilities than we should, but sometimes that is the way of mission work.

I also came to the realization that my own unhealed issues of the need to please people and the need to perform well had affected how I responded. Why did her words offend me *so much*? I did know, in my heart, that God was a loving Father, who loved me and accepted me as I was. So, why was it that I still got so wounded by another person's opinion of me? Why did it bother me that she said this in front of all my friends?

I had thought I was emotionally mature, but I started to realize that I still had unresolved issues in my life. I went to a few prayer counseling sessions for myself, to deal with lack of confidence and need to perform for acceptance. This emotional pattern was the result of a few extremely painful incidents in my life. I needed to recognize and confess my sin of unforgiveness toward those who had hurt me, and take their words and my wounds and leave them at the foot of the cross of Christ.

Being Equipped to Minister Effectively

The prayer counseling sessions that I attended helped me resolve some of my issues. I could also see how they would help our staff and those we were serving. Certainly, not every ministry will involve the people you are helping lashing out at you. If you are offering food and prayers, they are going to be glad to see you! But in any ministry where you get to know the people in more personal ways, painful confrontations will likely happen. I determined that we, as a staff, needed to learn more and become better equipped to minister to the wounded people we were trying to help.

There's a helpful, "user-friendly" course that addresses many of the basic issues that affect our emotional health called *Loved to Life*.[3] It can be taken online or in person at Life Center. Linda Forster, who is a qualified counselor, teaches this course. We encouraged almost our entire CFC staff to take the course. I recently asked Linda what would be a simple way to determine if you struggle with boundaries. She replied with a few nuggets of wisdom, "If you are working harder than the client for their healing, you have a poor boundary." And she added, "If you are lying awake nights, worrying about clients, that is taking too much responsibility for them and the situation." That's good advice.

Additional, intensive courses, such as an inner healing online course offered by Global Awakening, through their Christian Healing Certification Program, also provide practical instruction for learning how to administer inner healing. These trainings, along with others I have included in the recommended resources section, can prove to be useful when ministering to people from all walks of life. Many of the emotional wounds we experience have similar root issues. Learning about the effects of abuse and ways to respond to those who have been abused, started to help me actively listen and extend empathy in a better manner.

There was a woman who volunteered at the Center who helped with lunches and assisted the teachers. She was from the neighborhood where the Center was located. She did not have any children, but treated the Center kids like they were her own. She would get upset with me if I determined that a child needed to stay home for a day after behaving in a way that required serious consequences. She would often interrupt me and say that I was against a particular child—especially if it were a child that she knew personally. I listened to her, but in those early years, I probably wasn't actively listening. I didn't do a good job letting her know that I was hearing her concerns, and I found her distrust of my decisions to be frustrating.

After going to the *Elijah House Training for the Ministry of Prayer Counseling* classes, I started to understand her better. I knew this woman had a history of family abuse. I also knew that on a few occasions she had been the subject of police brutality. I started to realize that she did not trust *anyone* in authority to be looking out for the best for her, or especially for children. Why should she trust anyone, after all she had been through?

One day, as she was arguing with me—again—about a decision I made, I just looked at her and said, "I'm so sorry that the *authority figures* in your life let you down. I am so sorry that they could not be trusted."

She burst out into big heaving sobs. She hugged me and I let her cry on my shoulder. She said, "I'm so sorry, Miss Denise." I love this woman. To this day she is making big strides in her healing and is a help to others in the city.

The courses helped all of us start to look beyond the surface in our relationships with those we served. We learned to look more intently to find what might be behind some of the intense emotional outbursts that were sometimes displayed by the people that we worked with or were ministering to.

Learning about inner healing and being trained in prayer counseling will be invaluable to you as you go into consistent, compassionate ministry. After all, our goal in compassion ministry is to see people healed and set free. But for hidden wounds to be revealed it often requires God's intervention. And until a person is truly healed, any surface level progress will not be lasting. Healing comes with increased revelations of God's love and knowing His acceptance and forgiveness. Prayer counseling is a powerful tool in facilitating healing because the counselor turns to Jesus for His wisdom and healing during the sessions. Jesus is the true Healer. When we ask Him to move, He will, no matter how deeply wounded or how hurt the person. And with healing comes wholeness, joy and a changed life!

> OUR GOAL IN COMPASSION MINISTRY IS TO SEE PEOPLE HEALED AND SET FREE.

Reflection and Action

LISTEN

- "Song of Solomon" by Martin Smith

STUDY

- Romans 15:14 (AMP), Galatians 6:2-3, James 1:19, Ephesians 4:15, Romans 8:28-39 (TPT)

JOURNAL

1. Have you ever been wounded by someone you were trying to help? How did you react? What could you have done differently?

2. Do you have trouble with setting boundaries? In what way? Start considering ways you could improve this skill. What are they?

3. Are there areas in your life where you would like to see more personal growth? Check out the recommended resources to find materials that will help you grow.

CHAPTER 13

Wounded Leaders Wound Others

"Abba" (Arms of a Father) by Jonathan David Helser[1]

Leaders Ministering from an Orphan Spirit

Have you ever known an apparently compassionate pastor or ministry leader with an inspiring teaching gift, who turned out to be other than they seemed? When you interact with this leader, whether on committees, boards, special projects, or even as a staff member, a different picture of them emerges than the kind, caring one they project. The leader is overly demanding, controlling, and performance and works driven.

In staff meetings the leader becomes defensive and quickly irritated if someone questions their plans. The leader's goal is successful programs, measured in numbers. They expect results and give very little grace. Eventually some of the staff, despite still loving the congregation or the ministry, feel they need to step away from the leadership team. They can no longer endure being belittled and made to look like they are the problem. Unfortunately, some leave discouraged, dejected, less confident, and doubting their own abilities. Some feel so wounded by the experience that they get out of ministry work altogether.

Are these leaders particularly heartless, hypocritical, and egotistical? Or are they living a lonely, performance driven life with the identity of an "orphan spirit"? I believe it is the latter. The sad thing is that often the pastor or the leader is the last one to realize that they have a problem. They don't even realize the hurt they are causing others. In some ways their own woundedness, which is pushing them to be so performance oriented, has also blinded them to their effect on others.

I first heard the words "orphan spirit" several years ago, when Jack Frost, a minister and motivational speaker, taught at my church. A workshop on the topic was presented following his teaching. An orphan spirit was defined this way:

> The orphan spirit causes one to live life as if he does not have a safe and secure place in the Father's heart. He feels he has no place of affirmation, protection, comfort, belonging, or affection. Self-oriented, lonely, and inwardly isolated, he has no one from whom to draw Godly inheritance. Therefore, he has to strive, achieve, compete, and earn everything he gets in life. It easily leads to a life of anxiety, fears, and frustration.[2]

A person can experience living with an orphan spirit even if they grew up with a seemingly good father and/or mother. Perhaps their parent, or even another influential person in their life, showed love and approval only when they met overly high expectations. The parent cared, but thought tough love was the way to "make a man out of them." The person lived with a constant feeling of pressure to perform. When they did not meet some high standard, they faced ridicule and disapproval. They had no experience of unconditional love.

People can also be burdened by the orphan spirit if they had an absent father, who was not around to encourage them and not actually engaged with the family when he was home. Then those who have lived with abusive parents who administered extreme punishment often experience this identity issue as well. They lived in constant fear and learned to strive to please to avoid harm. All of these life situations can influence how a person sees themselves and how they show love and interact with others.

When a person with an orphan spirit becomes a leader, they operate out of a graceless, performance-oriented state of being. Often it takes a powerful encounter with God to reveal to their hearts that they are, in fact, a wounded soul themselves. They need a revelation of the Father's unconditional love and acceptance. There are many Christians who have accepted Christ's sacrifice for their lives but still see themselves as servants in the household, needing to follow all the rules and perform duties. They have not truly entered into their place as a son or daughter of the loving Father. I have heard several leaders tell of their journeys from slavery to sonship and the wonderful effect this transformation had in their lives, their families, and their ministry work.

Jack Frost's Story

During his teaching, Jack Frost taught us about the orphan spirit as he described his own life. Jack grew up with an overly demanding military father. He felt he could never please him, never be good enough, and never win his approval unless everything was done perfectly. His relationship with his father led him to rebel in his teen years and helped push him into a hard-living life as a sea captain when he was an adult.

Jack became a Christian in the 1980s, overcoming alcoholism and some other issues as he turned his life to God. However, he still did not know God as a loving Father. So, Jack went about trying to please God by being religious and strict about following the rules. He was a great speaker, but to his staff and close associates he was harsh, demanding, and easily irritated. His marriage also greatly suffered. He even treated his children similarly to the way he had been treated, always expecting a lot from them without extending much grace or affection.

Then in the mid-1990s, there was a tremendous outpouring of God's Spirit at a church in Canada. This outpouring continued for years. People were getting healed, delivered, and touched in many ways. Many experienced a revelation of God as the Father, who loves unconditionally. These God encounters happened so many times to so many people, tens of thousands in fact, that years later many people refer to this renewal/revival as "The Father's Blessing."

The revival revealed the great need for so many people, even ministry leaders, to experientially know God as their loving Father. This revelation was not for one group at one moment in time. It is a revelation revealed for all of us today, especially if we want to provide help to the hurting. We need to serve others out of love and not out of a performance or works mentality.

Jack was one of the leaders who had his whole life totally transformed in this outpouring. He found complete freedom from an orphan spirit during those God encounters at the conferences and personal prayer times that followed. One moment at the conference was particularly memorable. The speaker prayed, asking God to touch the men in the room so that they'd feel the Father's embrace. Jack found himself on the floor weeping.

> I felt as if God transported me back to a time when I was only ten years old. I suddenly saw vivid scenes of me as a child, hiding in a closet at night, fearful of the yelling and screaming I heard in my parents' room. I remembered the fear, the loneliness, and the sense of abandonment. I felt the deep, painful ache for my father's embrace—an embrace he was not able to give me during my childhood.
>
> Suddenly, I realized that now, 34 years later, my heavenly Father was meeting the deepest need in my heart for a natural demonstration of a father's affectionate love...As I lay on the floor weeping, Father God entered that dark closet of my childhood and held me in His arms. For 45 minutes, the Holy Spirit poured the love of God that the apostle Paul talked about through my mind, will, and emotions and washed away much of the guilt, shame, fear of failure and rejection, fear of intimacy, and the fear of love. My breakthrough finally came.[3]

I have heard numerous leaders speak about how their entire ministry was transformed as they encountered God's love, and embraced this understanding of Him as a loving Father. Jack described the changes he experienced in his ministry:

> As Father's love has brought restoration of intimacy to my marriage and family, it has changed my whole philosophy of ministry as well. I am no longer striving to be holy or to win God's favor. I don't want to do anything to hinder the intimate, loving relationship that God has given me. Ministry is no longer something that I have to work or strive for; comparisons, competition, and rivalry are fading away. Spiritual ambition is now but a shadow[4]

Jack Frost went to be with his Lord a number of years ago, but the ministry of inner healing that he and his wife, Trisha, started has continued and grown with the help of his children and staff. Shiloh Place Ministries provides a wealth of resources and counseling.

Finding Emotional and Spiritual Healing

Today, the revelation of the Father's heart is still greatly needed. God continues to unfold His unconditional, intimate love to people in so many ways. The orphan spirit is only one of many ways people experience emotional wounds. Wounds of abuse, wounds of injustice, and wounds of rejection are a few others. The revelation of the Father's Love has a way of healing so many of our hurts.

THE REVELATION OF THE FATHER'S LOVE HAS A WAY OF HEALING SO MANY OF OUR HURTS.

If you think that you struggle emotionally in some area that is affecting your life and those around you, I encourage you to tenaciously pursue healing. It may take some time to overcome years of feeling like an orphan, years of abuse, or years of other types of emotional wounding. Healing could start during an encounter with God at a worship service and through prayer from a ministry team. A few have had their lives totally changed, totally healed, in just one powerful encounter with God. But many others have found complete breakthrough with additional inner healing prayer counseling sessions.

Here are a few specific things you can do to pursue inner healing:

- Read several books on the topic of God as the loving Father.

- Search out scriptures that show or talk about God's Father love.

- Avail yourself of opportunities for inner healing prayer counseling offered in your area.

- Go online and avail yourself of some of the excellent online courses regarding inner healing.

- Go to places where you know God's presence can be encountered in worship and a ministry team is available to pray with you.

- Attend inner healing courses together as a staff.

- Take time off to travel to locations where personal ministry is available from experienced counselors over a period of several days. Churches who send staff to attend these retreats have found them to be instrumental in providing a healthy church atmosphere in many of their churches. Such intensive inner healing counseling would be especially helpful to staff of compassion ministries, since they are dealing with so many wounded people. It would be money well spent. An extensive section listing inner healing resources is provided at the back of this book under Recommended Resources.

I love how Jesus revealed God to the world as the Father who loves His sons and daughters so unconditionally, in ways they had never considered. The story of the prodigal son that Jesus tells in Luke 15:11-31 shows us a father so forgiving, so compassionate, and so in love with his son. This idea must have seemed mind blowing to these Jewish followers of the law. Few natural fathers have ever loved their children to such an extent. When you read these scriptures, you will notice how the father does not condemn the son or berate him for his foolish and sinful life. He welcomes him back without even requiring that he pay back all the money he wasted. The son thought that all he could ever hope to be was a servant. The father made it clear he was accepted as his son with full rights, not as a servant. Unfortunately, the older brother never realized that this kind of love had been available to him, all this time. He never approached his father as a son. He only saw himself as a servant slaving away, never enjoying life.

The foundation of inner healing comes from knowing Jesus as our Savior and Lord. He is the great Healer both physically and emotionally. Jesus tells us, *"The Spirit of the Lord is upon me, because He has anointed me to preach the gospel to the poor;* **he has sent Me to heal the brokenhearted***"* (Luke 4:18a, NKJV; emphasis mine).

Fall in love with Jesus, learn more about your own identify in His finished work, and pursue knowing the unconditional, amazing love of *The Father* in greater measure. Then, armed with a right understanding of being loved by God, go out and help a hurting world of wounded people who need to know that they no longer need to live like orphans. Their Abba Father is waiting to welcome them into His loving arms and into the family of God.

Reflection and Action

LISTEN

- "Abba" by Jonathan David Helser, on the *Beautiful Surrender* album

STUDY

- Read Luke 15:11-31 in different versions of the Bible, such as The Passion Translation and The Message. Notice the unconditional love of the Father. Notice the problem that the older brother had of not realizing that he was a son, instead of a servant.

- Read at least one book about God as a loving Father, even if you don't struggle with an orphan spirit. There are so many people in the world who don't know God as the unconditional loving Father. Learning more about this will help you minister to them.

JOURNAL

1. Do you see yourself as the son or daughter of the unconditional loving Father? Give examples of how you know this.

2. Do you identify with the older brother? Do you see yourself serving God and doing a lot of good works but not feeling the unconditional love of the Father? Write down some examples.

3. Do you see how not knowing our own worth or the unconditional love of God could affect what we expect of ourselves and others? Maybe you know someone in leadership dealing with this problem and could minister to them from the Father's Heart.

CHAPTER 14

The Power of Forgiveness

————————————————————————
"O Come to the Altar" by Elevation Worship[1]

Teaching Forgiveness

If there is one place on earth that I would call my happy place, it would be the beach—especially an uncrowded beach in North Carolina, with no boardwalks, just golden sea oats waving in the breeze. I usually take a book to read as I breathe in the salty fresh air and soak in the beauty. But I distinctly remember there was one time that I took my notes from a six-month counseling course that I had just finished. As I sat there in my usual happy place, I started to be quite unhappy.

I felt so helpless and discouraged as I reviewed my notes from the course.

Oh Lord, I sighed, *how are we ever going to help these inner-city families? How can we make any difference in the lives of these children?*

Each week of the course, the instructors had addressed different causes of deep inner wounds—sexual, physical and mental abuse, abandonment, parental inversion, depression, addictions—on and on the list went.[2]

I continued my prayer as I read further into my notes, *God, I don't know what to do. They have too many of these problems.*

The children and parents we worked with were not dealing with just one of these issues, but several of them. I knew our ministry was not equipped to be a counseling organization, nor was it our main mission.

We did have times where we talked, listened, and prayed with the children and parents about their concerns. But we just did not have the time or resources to address all of their deep inner wounds while running the after-school program. We had many positive alternative activities, academic help, parent dinners, and chapel times, but no real time devoted to in-depth counseling sessions.

I sat there on that beautiful beach feeling hopeless. How could we ever help our students and families get free of so much pain?

I'll never forget what God spoke to my heart that day. Even now I apply it to many situations in my life, including my own interpersonal relationships.

He said, "Teach them to forgive."

If we could teach them to forgive those who had hurt them, then God, in his amazing healing power, could begin the deep inner healing. This was such a wonderful answer to our dilemma. I thought, *Wow! We can do that*! We could make a point to discuss forgiveness with both the children and their parents on a regular basis.

Now, let me be clear. I do believe that long term counseling for inner healing definitely has its place. I even list numerous resources regarding inner healing in this book. Many people have found substantial freedom in their lives through counseling. But ours was not a counseling center. Still, it was important to address the hurting hearts of those who walked through our doors.

We started using the concept and practice of forgiveness as a basic building block for healing. We used it in disciplinary situations when two kids were fighting. We used it when talking to a single mother about the father who abandoned their child. We used it when teaching about parenting and addressing pain from a person's relationships with their own parents. As a staff, we also were conscious of asking for forgiveness and giving forgiveness. We talked about forgiveness a lot.

Forgiveness was a new concept for the children and their parents. In their experience in the inner city, revenge and an "an eye-for-an-eye" was the law of the land, which stemmed from the need to survive under extremely difficult circumstances. The first year I started the program, I told one mother in the housing projects that she might want to tell her son not to physically fight back over any little thing, and that it could save his life. She let me have it, reminding me that I was not from the "hood," and that I didn't know what I was talking about.

I remember some of the teen girls belting out, "She did this to me. I'm gonna get her back. You wait and see. After school. *Bring it!*" They would say it with a shake of their head from side-to-side and a hand waving in the air.

When I would mention forgiveness they would say, "Forgive her? What! No way, Miss Denise. What you talkin' bout? You crazy."

I wasn't, and neither were the rest of our staff. We remained determined to introduce this wonderful, amazing concept of *forgiveness* to these families. Eventually we saw some significant results. Many of the families saw great breakthrough because of choosing to forgive. Some of the parents and students even came to *us* and asked for forgiveness.

Jesus Modeled Forgiveness

Jesus was quite serious about our need to forgive others. He brings it up in what we call *The Lord's Prayer*. Matthew 6:12 says, *"and forgive us our sins, as we have forgiven those who sin against us."* Then He goes on to say in verse 14, *"If you forgive those who sin against you, your heavenly Father will forgive you. But, if you refuse to forgive others, your Father will not forgive your sins."*

That is some heavy stuff. We are saved by grace for sure, so what does this verse mean? There are a lot of unseen realities in the spiritual realm that keep us bound up in this world. Not forgiving others *gives the enemy legal right* to continue to taunt a person with what has been done to them. It causes a person to stay a victim. Unforgiveness is like keeping yourself tied to the perpetrator who offended you.

Forgiveness is not the same as acceptance, nor does it mean that what the other person did was not terribly wrong. It just means that you choose to let them go emotionally. You choose to not hold their sin against them or to seek revenge. (This does not mean you stop pursuing justice or even legal action if it is necessary.) We need to forgive, even if the other person does not acknowledge that they have done anything wrong. We must release the person, and let God deal with them, as we go on with our lives. We can even forgive people who have passed away.

Jesus modeled forgiveness. He forgave sinners. He forgave those who rejected Him and those who denied knowing Him. While He was hanging on that cross, being taunted by the Pharisees, the soldiers, and some in the crowd, He looked down on them and said, *"Father forgive them for they don't know what they are doing"* (Luke 23:34). When someone really hurts me, I try to remember this image of Jesus, totally innocent, being beaten and treated so badly. He chose to forgive. This gives me strength to also forgive. I am not innocent and perfect like Jesus. The least I can do is forgive another imperfect fellow human being. *When we choose to forgive, we are acting most like Jesus.*

> WHEN WE CHOOSE TO FORGIVE, WE ARE ACTING MOST LIKE JESUS.

One thing that helps enable us to forgive, is to know that those who cause great harm have suffered great harm. The abuser has usually been abused. With the help and love of Jesus, we can forgive. After all, *"love covers over a multitude of sins"* (I Peter 4:8b, NIV). I believe that forgiveness is a form of love because it brings

THE POWER OF FORGIVENESS | 147

freedom to someone who doesn't deserve it and brings freedom to the one doing the forgiving.

Consider the amazing, humbling scene at the Charleston, South Carolina courthouse.[3] Nine African America church members had been murdered in cold blood on June 17, 2015, after welcoming a newcomer to their Bible study. This misguided, racist, white supremacist shot them one by one. Yet several family members, who had lost loved ones, stood in that court telling this man, who had committed such a horrible act, that they forgave him. That was incredible. I don't know how the young man actually felt upon hearing this. He showed no remorse. But I do know one thing—those families will heal, and the legacy of their loved ones will continue.

At Center for Champions, we noticed a real difference in the lives of those around us when we started emphasizing the importance of forgiveness. After teaching more about forgiveness, praying with the CFC families, and showing them how to ask God to help them to forgive, we saw many of the parents and children find emotional healing. In addition, many were more willing to say they were sorry. Others then often responded with forgiveness. Although there was more work to be done, I'm happy to know that the new generation of leaders at the Center is continuing to teach forgiveness, and use this most important catalyst for emotional healing.

Forgiving Yourself

As some from the Center began to forgive those who hurt them, their hearts began to soften. They were starting to find breakthrough in several areas. However, they also started to be aware of their own faults and the ways that they had hurt others. We realized that they needed to also forgive themselves.

Jesus tells us to *"love your neighbor, as yourself"* (Mark 12:31). If you can't forgive yourself, how can you love yourself? If we can't forgive ourselves, then we become critical and judgmental of others. I know I, as a leader, had to forgive myself for areas that I believed I failed in or situations that I didn't handle very well.

Many of the people you will serve will need to forgive themselves. Some will come from pretty tough backgrounds and have areas in their lives where they feel shame and remorse. In order to experience freedom and a deeper awareness of the love of God, we have to bring our shame, our mistakes, and our sins and lay them at the feet of Jesus. There we receive His amazing grace and forgiveness, which in turn helps us to forgive and love ourselves. Then we have more than enough love to give to our neighbor.

I saw the power of forgiving oneself demonstrated one night when I was on a mission trip to England. Our team went to a small church where Georgian Banov was speaking. When we walked into the sanctuary, the music was playing and people were enthusiastically celebrating God. Most were singing, and some were even dancing. It was a lively bunch, but one exceedingly tall man—with his arms crossed and a scowl on his face—stood out like a sore thumb. He did not enter into any expression of worship, not even singing. Instead he looked like he was probably wondering what was wrong with all of these crazy people.

As the teaching was finished, I came up to the front as part of the ministry team to help pray for people who desired it. But, as I stood there, my eyes kept drifting to the back of the room, where the tall man was still leaning against the back wall. I felt that God wanted me to pray for him.

So, I did something unusual. I left the stage and walked to the back of the room. I felt this strong sense that God wanted me to minister to this man, even if he did not come up for prayer. I first prayed for the guy beside him, so it didn't look like I was singling him out. The other guy was happy to receive prayer. Then I just moved to the next person, which was "Mr. Grump." I felt a little lump in my throat as I approached this man, because I didn't know what I was supposed to say to him. I had no words, no mental picture, just a feeling that God wanted to talk to him.

I hesitated for a second, and then, strained my neck as I looked up into his face. (I am five feet two inches tall and this man had to have been six feet seven inches or more.) He still had his arms crossed, and he still had a scowl on his face. He did not look me in the eye. The first thing I said was, "You're a really big guy." (Here's a little tidbit about prophetically praying for people: sometimes you have to "prime the pump" with love in your heart. You just start saying something kind, then God will give you the words to say.)

Now, the words just started to flow as I said, "But I see you sitting on the Father's lap like a little boy. God loves you very much."

I could *feel* so much compassion and love for this man, whom I did not even know. I knew it was God's heart for him that I was feeling. By now, he was looking at me, his face softened, somewhat. Then I said something I had never said to anyone. But since this was a mission trip, I was emboldened to speak what I felt the Father was saying.

"You've done a lot of bad things in your life."

By now, the man had unfolded his arms, and was looking at me intently.

"But God has forgiven you of all those things. You are a totally new person in Christ. That old man is dead. You are a new creation."

After saying that, I paused to see if there was more to say, and I felt there was still something missing. Then, I heard these thoughts from the Father, "He hasn't forgiven himself."

So, I looked up again at this big guy, who was now intrigued and attentive, and said, "God has forgiven you, but you haven't forgiven yourself. God wants you to forgive yourself."

A tear started to trickle down his weathered face. I knew that the Father had touched his heart. I then moved away, to let him soak in God's message himself. I was so thankful that God had directed me to bring a message of the Father's love to his heart.

I walked back up front and prayed for a few more people. I noticed that this man had come away from the back of the room. He had moved up to the front and was now walking along with a line of people, going through what some call a "spiritual fire tunnel." This is where a person walks between two rows of people. Those people may gently touch the head or shoulder of the person and pray a quick blessing for each one, as they walk through. The Holy Spirit often touches lives. There can be many expressions of joy as people pass through. (It's really God's children having fun.)

A few minutes later, I heard an announcement that someone's back had been healed. I looked, and it was "Mr. Ex-Grump," healed and laughing, and joining in the fun. The change in him all started when I delivered the message from the Father's heart, the message that God loved him, had forgiven him, and now wanted him to forgive himself. Forgiveness brought both emotional and physical healing!

THE CHANGE IN HIM STARTED WHEN I DELIVERED THE MESSAGE FROM THE FATHER'S HEART

The Bible says in Psalms 103:12 that, *"He has removed our sins as far from us as the east is from the west."* East never meets west. Give Grace, Grace, Grace, to others and to yourself. Then tell the world this wonderful healing message of *forgiveness.*

Reflection and Action

LISTEN

- "O Come to the Altar" by Elevation Worship

STUDY

- Matthew 5:23-24, Matthew 6:9-15, Matthew 18:21-35, Luke 23:34, Colossians 3:12-13

JOURNAL

1. Are their people in your life that you need to forgive? Write down their names and ask the Father to help you forgive. If possible let these people know you forgive them. If the person is no longer alive, ask a friend to witness you speak out-loud that you forgive that person who wounded you and are sorry for any pain you caused them. Amazingly this substitutionary action can bring lasting healing.

2. Are their people that you have wounded that you should ask to forgive you? What efforts are you willing to make to reconcile?

3. If you are not able to do the first two, then perhaps you might want to seek out some type of inner healing counseling and read several of the books about forgiveness listed in the recommended resources.

GOD HAS FORGIVEN YOU, BUT YOU HAVEN'T FORGIVEN YOURSELF. GOD WANTS YOU TO FORGIVE YOURSELF.

CHAPTER 15

Don't Quit 'Til You're Done

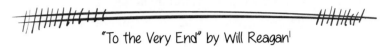

"To the Very End" by Will Reagan[1]

God's Intervenes to Keep Me from Quitting

The phone rang. I was surprised to hear the voice of a friend I hadn't heard from in a few years. She was not a let's-go-get-coffee-and-chat kind of friend but more of a kick-you-in-the-butt exhorter. A mighty prayer warrior, she had prayed and believed for our mission since the founding of Center for Champions.

She started the conversation by saying, "Denise, how's the Center for Champions going?"

Choking back tears, I responded with my own question, "Did someone call you?"

"No," she responded.

Just that week, my program director, had informed me that he and his wife were moving out of state. I totally understood their reasons for leaving. The move would absolutely be best for their family. But, personally, it seemed like devastating news. They were loving, talented people, and a crucial part of the ministry. I had envisioned someday turning the ministry completely over to them. This turn of events had me considering closing the Center for Champions for good. Eight years is a long time in urban ministry, and I was tired. I had known many others who had started out and moved on to other things in less time.

This is where my thoughts had been when I picked up the phone that day. My friend continued on the phone and said:

> Listen, I was having shoes put on my horse and I was listening to the man talking as he was doing the job. But, all of a sudden, the man faded away and I had an open vision. I never had an open vision *this* clear before. In the vision, I was on the corner of a street in the inner city of Harrisburg, talking to a group of boys who were about ten years old. They were asking me about my daughter's radio show. I looked over and saw you standing there, smiling at the boys. All of a sudden, God said very emphatically, "Call Denise and encourage her. Tell her she's My heart touching those that many will not go to. Tell her all Heaven is with her." I am calling you to tell you about this vision.

I was absolutely stunned. I told her the circumstances of how I was thinking of quitting and how much I needed this prophetic word on *that* day. She told me to keep going, and then said goodbye. (I told you she wasn't a chit-chat kind of person.)

Later, I kept thinking about that open vision, and how God had said that I was *"His heart touching others that many won't go to"*—that just wrecked me. I contemplated, *Oh my sweet Lord, am I really Your heart touching others?* And thought about those words, *"all Heaven is with her."* I knew immediately that I could not quit. He was asking me to stay. How could I not?

I also knew instinctively, however, that this vision was not really about me. It reminded me just how much God loved these needy and sometime rebellious inner-city kids and their parents—and how He would go to great lengths to be sure they heard of His love and received spiritual and practical help.

Consider the words: "His heart touching those *that many will not go to.*" Unfortunately, not many people are willing to come and serve in the inner cities of America. Many don't see the pain, the despair, the injustice, the poor role models, and the results of fatherlessness that are behind the anger and poor decisions. Once again, God was reminding me that *He sees.* His heart hears the cry of those that are often forgotten.

That's how God feels about all the hurting people in the world, not just those in the inner city. Who will go to help the combative autistic teen? Who will continue to counsel that alcoholic who's "fallen off the wagon" – again? Hurting people, everywhere, need to see Jesus with "skin on." *They need people to stay and not give up on them.*

I can't promise you that God will send someone with an open vision to tell you not to give up. But He will find a way to reach you and encourage you, if you will be open to hear. I needed a message I could not explain away. Sometimes, we have made up our mind and we filter what we hear to fit what *we want* to do. Please don't do that. Be honest and let God speak whatever He wants to speak. He might speak to you through a scripture, a word of counsel, or the testimony of a changed life. He speaks, but we have to be listening.

> THEY NEED PEOPLE TO STAY AND TO NOT GIVE UP ON THEM.

Fortunately, God faithfully provided a new program director. I found out that there was a qualified young man who had recently moved into the area. For eight years, Richie did a tremendous job serving as the CFC director. He grew to love the families of the inner city. He started his own street ministry and healing outreach while still working at the Center. Now, he has formed the Capital Area Dream Center. This one facility houses many programs that serve the needy and also is a place to coordinate citywide outreaches and networking between organizations. I like to think that by my not quitting CFC and instead hiring this young man (who was recently out of Bible college), he gained experience and became better prepared for what he is doing now.

If you are called to be involved in a compassion ministry in some capacity, know that God will be with you. He will not ask you to keep on doing what is difficult to do, without helping you. He will provide the resources, bring new ministry team and staff members, and perhaps even give you prophetic words or let you hear great testimonies to encourage you. God knows you and how you are made. He will encourage you in the mountain-top experiences and in the valleys, calling out, "Keep going, you've got this!"

Love Does the Hard Things

In the first year that we were discussing starting Center for Champions, I met with a local pastor named Dave Hess. He made this statement that stuck with me for many years, "*I wonder how many people have gone to their grave having not seen their dreams fulfilled, because they were not willing to do the hard work to make it happen.*"[2] Ministry takes tenacity and hard work. God needs people willing to do the hard things. *Love does the hard things.* Any mother or father can attest to that.

Jesus never promised us a life without challenges. He promised us joy. He promised us peace but He said there would be difficulties (John 16:33). I'll be honest, I'm a comfort loving girl. I would relish an easy life—devoid of difficulties and challenges. But, I love Him more than I love my own comfort. Jesus' example provokes me to press past my feelings.

> *And let us run with endurance the race God has set before us. We do this by keeping our eyes on Jesus, the champion who initiates and perfects our faith. Because of the joy awaiting him, he endured the*

cross...Think of all the hostility he endured from sinful people; then you won't become weary and give up.
(Heb. 12:1b-3)

Compassion ministry work can be difficult. There are the daily programs and team management responsibilities to run. There are times when the funds seem quite low. The needs of the people you want to serve are often overwhelming and far greater than you or your ministry's ability to meet them. Helping people is not simple. You are tackling long standing cultural problems; and face the unseen forces of the enemy, who is not willing to let go of those held captive for so long. He uses oppressing and depressing tactics to stop you and your team. Sometimes the people you are helping make choices that negate the advantages you were attempting to give them. In addition, if you are ministering to children and youth it may take years to see obvious results, if you see them at all.

These challenges not only affect the leaders of ministries but can influence and weigh on any people who are serving consistently, whether as a staff member in a compassion ministry or as a faithful volunteer.

All of these tasks and struggles can start to wear you down. At times you feel alone and that no one understands the pressures you face. You can become depressed and you might want to give up and quit. Ministry is *hard* and requires great sacrifice.

Ministry People May Get Depressed

It seems to me that many people who serve in compassion ministry are exceptionally passionate. That's good because passion motivates them to take action. But sometimes passionate people tend to experience significant emotional ups and downs. I've read several books that describe amazing missionaries who sometimes got despondent. A. W. Tozer describes this phenomenon beautifully:

It is characteristic of the God-intoxicated, the dreamers and mystics of the Kingdom, that their flight-range is greater than that of other men. Their ability to sweep upward to unbelievable heights of spiritual transport is equal only by their sad power to descend, to sit in dazed dejection by the River Chebar or to startle the night watches with their lonely grief.[3]

Have you ever read the story of Elijah found in 1 Kings 19? He became so depressed that he wanted to die. He had challenged and taken down all of the false prophets and Jezebel was out to kill him. He felt alone, not knowing of any others who had not bowed to Baal. In 1 Kings 19:4 Elijah tells God he gives up, "*Then he went on alone into the wilderness, traveling all day. He sat down under a solitary broom tree and prayed that he might die. 'I have had enough, Lord,' he said. 'Take my life, for I am no better than my ancestors who have already died.'*"

Are you getting this? This mighty prophet was so discouraged he wanted to die! He then falls asleep. God doesn't chastise him for being so depressed. Instead He sends him an angel who wakes him up, and provides him with water and baked bread. (*It never hurts when having an emotional meltdown to consider whether you need sleep, and what you have or have not eaten.*)

Later, Elijah goes up and hides in a cave. God sends a fierce windstorm, an earthquake, and then a fire. Yet God is not speaking in any of those dramatic ways. Instead, He sends a gentle whisper. He tells Elijah that he's not alone and gives him some specific instructions about who to anoint as his successor to become the next spiritual leader.

An encouraging scene unfolds as Elijah puts his mantle on the young man, Elisha, who was willing to join him (1 Kings 19:21). I love that God recognized that Elijah desperately needed others to help carry his load. I still remember the day I finally decided to believe for the money to pay someone to be my administrative assistant. God did provide the funds and I had several wonderful assistants over the years that brought much joy to my service at the Center.

It's Okay to Take a Rest

In addition to having times where you need to rely on other people, there may come a time when you just need to *take a break or take an extended rest away from the ministry.* Traditional missionaries take furloughs. Perhaps other types of ministry leaders in America should also. Of course, that could mean you need to find the right person to keep things going long enough for the leader to take a break. If a break is needed, I am confident that God will supply the necessary help. If turning the ministry over to someone else isn't feasible but the leader severely needs a break, perhaps it would be wise to even close the program temporarily.

Why is it so hard for some of us to realize that we can stop for a little while and rest and the world won't fall apart? The ministry will survive if you take time off, and even if activities and programs have to be reduced or stopped for a season. Wendy Walters, a motivational speaker and book publisher, says:

> I have often counseled others, "Rest is a strategy." I have not often taken my own counsel. For high achievers or high nurturers, for those with vast commitments and those with a fear of failure, rest is a threat. Rest is for lucky or lazy people, but it is definitely not a luxury in which they can indulge.
>
> Not so. Rest is for you. Rest is for me. It is God's gift. He promises to come to you when you rest.[4]

Wendy then quotes from Eugene Peterson's wonderful idiomatic translation of scripture that addresses the topic of rest so well:

> *Are you tired? Worn Out? Burned out on religion? Come to me. Get away with me and you'll recover your life. I'll show you how to take a real rest. Walk with me and work with me—watch how I do it.*

Learn the unforced rhythms of grace. I won't lay anything heavy or ill-fitting on you. Keep company with me and you'll learn to live freely and lightly.
(Matt. 11:28-30 MSG)

Rest is a place in the heart and mind. But sometimes it actually involves reduced activity. I wish I had thought of just taking a long rest when I was running CFC. Instead, I "retired" two times before I actually finished my time at CFC because it never occurred to me to just *take a break or a rest*. I thought the only way to not be in charge and responsible for so many things was to quit. The first time I stepped down, my father was dying and my husband needed to have heart surgery. My family absolutely needed my undivided attention. Nine months later when we were in need of an executive director, again, I was ready to return. The second time I "retired," which was in 2011, I had contracted Lyme disease and was getting too tired and too ill to carry on. This time we turned the executive director position over to a capable young woman, while I remained an officer on the board.

> REST IS A PLACE IN THE HEART AND MIND.

Center for Champions Almost Ended

In 2013, Center for Champions was facing financial difficulties. In addition, the executive director decided to pursue a different career path. It was a wise and beneficial move for her, as she started using her other talents producing beautiful hand-crafted pottery. We began wondering about the future of CFC. The board discussed the possibility of closing CFC for good, after fifteen years of operation. We were several thousand dollars in debt with few ideas of how to keep the program going.

As the board president and founder of the program, I knew that making the decision to close would have been the easier path. But I didn't feel God telling us to do that. I kept thinking of the good things happening. Shannon, a talented and compassionate new staff member, was mentoring several teens and Linda was still ministering to the parents. I suggested that we at least try to keep the teen program and a few other fruitful programs going. I didn't want to see it end if it wasn't God's will. We needed to hear from Him.

God answered our prayers with a miraculous provision. Several months before this, we had applied for a Wells Foundation grant. (We often applied for grants, big and small, but seldom received any. And when we got the rare grant, it was small.) One day, while I was at home, I got a call from the man administering the Wells Foundation grant. He asked my name and began telling me that CFC had just been awarded a *$25,000* grant for our teen program.

He asked, "Where should I mail the check?"

I was shocked and asked cautiously, "Uh, what kind of paper work or requirements are there to receive this grant?"

I asked because a board member had written the grant application and I really didn't know what we'd be required to do. With our financial limitations and our plan to have less staff, I didn't know if we could meet their requirements.

The man said in a matter-of-fact tone, "Well, just send us an overview of your work at the end of next year, when you apply again."

I could hardly believe my ears. *What foundational grant gives you $25,000 with no strings attached and no paperwork and tells you to apply next year!* I tried to remain composed. I heard myself responding slowly and guardedly, in my best professional and sweet melodious Southern voice, "Well, we'll be sure to do that." I thanked him calmly, but profusely, telling him how this grant would mean so much to our teens and how it was such an answer to prayer.

But as soon as I hung up that phone, I was punching the air, giggling, and doing my happy dance, screaming and thanking God over and over. Later that summer, others gave generously and all our debt was paid. (Yep, that's My Daddy.)

A Most Difficult Last Year

Since we had the money to pay a few staff, and I was able to work pro bono, I agreed to come back as executive director, but only for one last year. I returned in the summer of 2013. The 2013/2014 school year turned out to be a difficult period with lots of "drama." Just in the first month a staff person had to leave due to family needs, an angry student broke glass panels in the church door, and our bus required expensive repairs.

Then, as the school year progressed, a few angry parents confronted staff, and I took the brunt of it. Confusion about requirements for a county grant caused staff misunderstandings and other relationship problems also arose. In the *Praise as Warfare* chapter, I mentioned that one particular year would best be described as "the year from hell." Well, 2013/2014 turned out to be the sequel. Looking back now, I think the enemy just couldn't believe that he had not succeeded in closing us down, so he was doing everything he could to try to stop us again.

One day, I was almost out of my mind with the many frustrations. So, I took a drive to watch a successful basketball/mentoring program. I was so close to telling that director, who I respected and had known for a long time, to please just take over our ministry. But after learning how much they had going on, I realized they already had their hands full. If they did take on CFC, CFC's mission would not be fulfilled and it would just become one of their many programs. I'm glad I didn't ask them to take over CFC. I had not heard God's direction to do that. I was just ready to give up. Why am I telling you this long, woeful story? Because when we hit a rough spot I think it's helpful to hear what others have endured and how they pressed through.

The Fruit of Persevering

Not long after the day when I almost threw in the towel, I met with a talented and qualified man named Jeff, who had a desire in his heart to start his own mentoring ministry in the inner city. I happened to call him at the very same time that he had been praying and seriously seeking for God's direction. We met several times to discuss the possibility of him taking over the ministry of Center for Champions. It quickly became clear that he was the right person to continue CFC. He had a vision for mentoring and was ready to wholeheartedly commit to the success of the Center. The staff was now set and the board knew the ministry was going to be in good hands. In May 2014, I gladly turned the Center over to them.

Despite all the difficulties that year, some wonderful things also happened. That year, several former students, who had graduated from high school, came back to teach the dance class for the younger girls. Our team danced at Christmas, a neighborhood block party, and even at the teen program director's wedding!

During that same 2013-2014 school year, we met a new mother who lived in the inner city and enrolled her girls in our program for the first time. Here are some of her words given as a testimony for our *Center for Champions 2014 Summer Newsletter*:

> *There is not enough time in the world, or paper, for me to express the impact Center for Champions has had on my life and the life of my family. Center for Champions was there for us during an extremely rough patch this past year, both financially and spiritually, and there is no way I could ever feel I have repaid the program and its employees for their generosity. When I first signed my girls up for the program I simply expected Center for Champions to help keep my girls focused on homework and to help keep them busy after school. But oh boy has Center for Champions done WAY more than that!!! With the help of Shannon...we have gone from a very non-Christian family to a family*

that embraces the love God has for us and the awesome people he has brought into our lives. Christ has also worked through Ms. Denise and the wonderful parent dinners helped me see that living the Christian life can help me be a better parent for all my children, those involved in the program and those that are not.

If we had closed CFC the summer of 2013, this new family wouldn't have received our help. Quitting that summer would have been like running a long marathon and not finishing the race when the goal line was just around the corner. I prayed for so many years for the right person to take over CFC, and I almost gave up right before I met him. I was only a month away from our first meeting, when I considered asking the program director of that basketball program to take the ministry from me.

I praise God that many children and their families continue to be helped through the ministry of CFC. *My Jesus* is smiling that someone else is being *His heart* helping these inner-city boys and girls, who so need to be affirmed and mentored, and still reaching out to the parents, who desperately need a helping hand.

Maybe my experience will help you hang in there through the challenging times. I really want to say, *"Don't quit 'til you're done!"* If you need to, take a rest. Listen to wise counsel, but be sure to bring the question back to the Lord in prayer. Don't leave until God provides clear confirmation to your heart that you've completed your run and it's the right time to go.

Reflection and Action

LISTEN

- "To the Very End" by Will Reagan and United Pursuit

READ

- Acts 2:14-18, 1 Kings 19 (MSG), Matthew 11:28-30 (check out several versions)

JOURNAL

1. Have you ever felt like giving up on something? Did you resolve to persevere? Or did you give up? If you persevered, what helped you decide to stay?

2. If you are having a difficult time right now, list some things that you think might help you cross the finish line.

3. Do you have a hard time resting in God? What makes it so hard for many of us to let things go and just rest? What can you do to find more opportunities to rest in the Lord?

... COME TO ME. GET AWAY
WITH ME AND YOU'LL RECOVER
YOUR LIFE. I'LL SHOW YOU HOW
TO TAKE A REAL REST ...
MATTHEW 11:28-30, MSG

SECTION V

Renewing Your Strength & Preventing Burnout

CHAPTER 16

The Power of Praise in the Midst of Warfare

"Blessed Be Your Name" by Matt Redman[1]

The Most Difficult Year

Worship music has the power to help strengthen us, keep us focused on God, renew our resolve, and lift us off the mat when we are down for the count. There was one particular day that worship turned my mourning into dancing. And the enemy met defeat. First, I'd like to explain the story behind the mourning.

Five years after starting the CFC, I drove to the Center a few hours before the program began, and parked in the church parking lot. I was alone; no one else had arrived. I usually parked my car beside our eleven-passenger van. *Where is the van?* I wondered. *It's always parked here.* I began to mull over in my mind what could have happened to it. *Did someone take it to get fixed? Hmmm. Oh no, did someone steal it?!*

Now, you must understand that this was not a valuable van. Ceiling material was falling down, paint was peeling, and there were dents and BB or possibly bullet holes in the sides. The teens in the program would jokingly say they were too embarrassed to be seen riding in this van. But it was all we had and our finances were low.

We *needed* the van, that day, to pick up the kids from various schools. *Where is our van?* I anxiously wondered. Then I realized, *Oh no, the driver must have stolen it, because he was so mad about being fired.* (I had been forced to terminate the bus/van driver's employment and he had not been happy about it.) And, as I considered the possibility that he could have stolen the van, I began having what could best be described as a full-blown tantrum, tears and all, in my car. Fortunately, it was just me and God in there. But, before I continue with what eventually happened, I want to explain why a 50-year-old woman might respond in such an immature, "out of my mind" way. You see, the missing van was only the most recent problem that the CFC staff and I had faced that school year.

Even now, as I think about it, that school year could most accurately be called "The Year from Hell." The month before the start up in the fall, the compassionate, resourceful young father of three, who was the middle-school class teacher and our bus/van driver, informed us that his growing family required he find a full-time job that paid him at least enough to live on. I totally understood and released him to go. *But now what to do?* I thought. I had two positions to fill—a teacher for teens and a driver.

An intern I trusted recommended a man he had gotten to know who could be our driver. His license and clearances passed, and so he was hired. I also hired an African American pastor to teach the middle school preteens and teens. I thought that they would surely listen to this man and that he would be a great role model. But the first day, he sent eight misbehaving youth to my office. It became increasing clear that he was not used to disrespectful, hardened inner-city teens. Within two weeks, he had found another part-time job in the school district, with better pay and less stress.

So, now I had to step in to fill his void. I was already not only the executive director—doing promotion, filling out forms and all that business-like stuff—but also the daily program director, which was sort of like acting as a principal in our after-school program that served about fifty kids. Suddenly, I had to be one of the teachers, too.

The first three days that I took over teaching the middle school class, I loved it. I thought to myself, *Yes, this is what I really love. I love teaching young people that God has great plans for their lives. I love trying to inspire and give them hope. Isn't this what got me into doing this ministry, anyway?* But, unfortunately, homework also needed to get done and soon these particular kids, that year in this class, were not that interested in anything this old lady was telling them to do.

One day in this class, it just seemed that the teens came in with bad attitudes from the start. There was continuous back and forth chatter as they "busted" on each other. Then they ganged-up on me when I tried to get them to participate in class. "F—k you Ms. Denise." "No, I will not sit down! *B-h!*" Even one teen boy, who was usually reasonable, got caught up in his friend's attitude. When I asked him to go work on the computer, he said: "I'm going to pop you." All the kids laughed. Big talk, big attitude, big disappointed me. I will tell you right now, classroom management in the urban setting is not something I ever mastered. And that was the last time I tried to be a teacher in the program. I quickly searched for someone to teach instead of me.

That same day, when we were releasing the kids to go home, a fight broke out outside between two twelve-year-old boys. One boy was someone we had had to permanently suspend but he came back to hang out in the church yard. He was picking a fight with one of the nicer, more respectful guys. Then I, without too much thought (and I would not recommend this), jumped in the middle to try to stop the fight from becoming physical. I had just learned a new trick at a seminar in dealing with combative students and it came in handy. I grabbed the reasonable guy's arm and bent it behind him, as he went to punch the hardened guy. It actually worked! Both boys were a few inches taller than my five feet two inches, so this was not that smart. But, I knew if the gentler, nicer boy hit the downright mean and violent guy, he could get seriously hurt. We'd have a real problem. Thankfully my action diffused the situation.

While I was dealing with this situation, a father of one of our girls had arrived to pick up his daughter. He saw what was happening and tried to tell the boys to be respectful. I herded the students onto the van to go home. It seemed as if things were under control as the father walked his daughter to their car, but he got a glimpse of another fight about to start. Another boy was about to punch a different kid. So, he blocked the punch with his arm and held the boy's arm for just a second, telling him to calm down and stop. Then he left with his daughter. He was a sweet man with a sweet daughter. On that day they were like a life-preserver God threw to me in the midst of the storm. It will be critical to look for this kind of God-sent help when you're involved in ministry.

What a day! But the frustration was not over. A half hour later the phone rang and there on the end of the line was the mother of the boy in the van, the boy who had been stopped from punching the other child. She was angry at me and started cussing me out (fortunately some was in Spanish so I didn't understand). She wanted to know who put his hands on her boy, referring to the father who had stopped the punch. I numbly said something about his blocking the swing to avoid a fight and then added something like, "If you only knew the things your kids put me through today. I'm not going to talk about it now. Goodbye."

I hung up the phone, put my face in my hands and just cried. I wish I could say this was a rare day, but we did have several other days that were almost this bad in the course of the many years I was with the Center.

Let me interject here, lest you judge these youth as terrible thugs or the moms as ungrateful. Our program was not like The Achiever's Club, which was an excellent program in the city reaching the "cream-of-the-crop" youth. Ours was geared to the academically average, or often even below-average youth, the ones most likely to drop out of school. These kids were the ones who sometimes got suspended at school. Each one of the children and teens who were being difficult that day had no fathers in their lives. Many had fathers in prison. Some had never known their fathers at all.

Fortunately, these youths did, at least, have one parent or guardian who wanted a better life for their children. They were willing to sign them up for our program and come to our required family dinners. However, some of the parents had had poor role models themselves. So, when the children acted disrespectfully, they thought they might get away with it, and *a few* of the parents would respond defensively to any disciplinary action. The parents had learned to live in survival mode. Plus, unfortunately, the whole culture of the urban city schools was known for trash talk. On top of all that, as mentioned, I was not gifted in alternative classroom management. I am sure I didn't handle the situation in the most skillful way.

Turning Mourning into Dancing

So, what do these situations have to do with the van getting stolen? I'm getting there.

We were understaffed, behavior problems were out of control, and my emotions were on edge. To top it off, the intern who had referred the van/bus driver, called me. He said he had reliable information that our bus driver had resorted to taking drugs *again*. (I wish I had known that history before I had hired him.) He said that I should tell him he couldn't drive that day, but not say why. *Huh? How do I do that?* And I should let him go. Fire him. *Oh goodness.* After the call, I had a reasonable talk with the driver. I did finally reveal what our suspicions were and our need to let him go. He didn't have much money and probably needed the job. He was not a happy camper, to say the least.

So, the day that I was having my tantrum was the culmination of months of a very, very difficult year. I sat in my car. Frankly, I felt like it was the last straw. I couldn't take it anymore. *How were we going to pick up the students that day from the schools?* I sobbed and cried out to God with my usual prayer, *Lord please send someone else to do this job!* I turned on the stereo in my car and a song from the last CD I had played resounded through the car. It was the song by Matt Redman called "Blessed Be Your Name."[2]

At first, I listened to calm myself down, but then I kept pushing the repeat button over and over. The words that particularly caught my attention were those reminding us to bless God even when the sun isn't shining, even when we're experienced suffering, even when our offering to God comes with pain. It's a song of declaration that says I will bless God no matter what the circumstances! It fed my soul, helping take my focus off my problems and onto His goodness and worthiness of praise. By now, I was standing alone, outside my minivan, with the door wide open. I cranked that song up as loud as it would go.

The parking lot, located across the street from the church where Center for Champions met, was in an area called South Allison Hill. This area had been designated by many groups as having the most crime and the highest percentage of impoverished families, with the most children. In fact, when we moved our program into that old church building, on that particular street, our insurance agent said that was a terrible area of town. I laughed and said, "Well, that's what we do. We go to the worst areas that need help." Even some of our parents would not look for housing on that street. It was just too dangerous to live there.

Standing in that parking lot where weeds were pushing up through the cracked pavement, amidst the trash, the cigarette butts, the broken glass, and the who-knows-what-else. Run-down buildings with broken, graffiti-painted windows surrounded me. Despite all this, I began to dance to Matt Redman's song. Dance and sing and praise God, right in the middle of the day. There were not many people around. But I didn't care either way. An older gentleman with dark leathery skin was sitting on his front porch directly across the street, watching me curiously. I think he was probably asking himself what that crazy white lady was doing. I didn't care, and besides, in the inner city you can do just about anything and people simply look the other way. So, I smiled at him and waved and went on about my dancing.

I won a huge victory that day. I can even feel it today as I sit here writing. This was one of those monumental, *build-an-altar* days. I sacrificed my praise there in that parking lot. The enemy did not defeat me. He did not defeat the Center. I was not going to quit. I had been drawn to praise *My Jesus,* drawn by His Loving Spirit, as I listened to that song. I was drawn to praise Him, once again, by remembering our history together. I knew from experience His great faithfulness to me, to the other staff, and to the families we served at the Center.

But the story isn't completely finished yet. After that episode of praise (or hilarity, or maybe reaching a point of being *out of my mind*), I walked around the corner of the church that faced 13th Street. Our basement entrance was on that side. And can you believe it? *There* was our van! What!? He hadn't stolen the van! He had just parked it on this other street, a place where we never parked it. I burst out laughing so hard at myself and my extreme drama over *nothing.*

I chuckled at just how far I had let my "pretty little head" go to the depths of despair, when I was sure our van had been stolen. And all the while it had been sitting here around the corner, just barely out of view. I think it was a test, a God test, and I passed it. I looked up to the heavens and smiled. I knew God was having a great laugh at his little drama queen daughter, having a tantrum over *nothing*. We shared a precious moment.

But that day I learned something. I learned that in the face of trials and tribulations, real or *perceived*, I was able to praise Him and find joy and strength through worship.

Praise and Dancing Bring Victory

Praise, even to the point of dancing, will be one of your greatest tools against the enemy's attacks. Don't go into battle without it.

I'm not the only one who dances and praises God over my troubles. A friend of mine, when speaking at a women's retreat, taught about the power of doing just that. She told a story of going through the rooms in her house and dancing over the troubles her family was experiencing. In time, her family experienced their sweet victory! I particularly like that it drives the devil crazy, especially when we dance in the midst of difficult times. It proves he has not won and that God is still on His throne.

The Bible gives us great examples of times when worship was the key to victory. Miriam and the women danced, declaring the victory God had won for them over their enemies. David famously danced with all his might, embarrassing his wife by his wild abandonment in worship. When Saul was having demonic attacks, he'd call for David to just play music and the demons would flee. In the N.T. we find Paul and Silas in prison, yet they choose to worship and sing to the Lord. Then, God brought a great deliverance. (See Exod. 15:20, 2 Sam.6:16, 1 Sam. 16:23 and Acts 16:25-26.)

Jehoshaphat faced an army so much greater than his own, that was coming to destroy Judah. The Israelites had no chance at all. They fasted, prayed, and turned their hearts toward God. He replied that they would not even have to fight the battle. Their battle plan became sending out the worship team.

> *This is what they sang: "Give thanks to the LORD; his faithful love endures forever!" At the very moment they began to sing and give praise, the Lord caused the armies of Ammon, Moab, and Mount Seir to start fighting among themselves* (2 Chron. 20:21b-22).

Never stop dancing and singing and praising the Lord. He loves to see you take those difficult situations and turn things around. As your dance and sing, your voice and your song become a sacrifice of praise. I include song titles with each of the chapters to encourage you to make your own playlist. I hope they will be an encouragement to you, as they have been to me. You are bringing light where darkness has reigned before. There will be warfare. Come prepared with the weapons of praise.

Reflection and Action

LISTEN

- "Blessed Be the Name" by Matt Redman

STUDY

- 2 Samuel 6:12-21 (NLT), 2 Chronicles 20: 1-30 (NLT), Acts 16:16-34, Psalm 73

JOURNAL

1. If you still haven't done so, start making a playlist that includes some of the songs that begin each chapter. Or create your own playlist of songs that you like that pertain to the chapter topics.

2. Read Psalm 77. The writer changes from depressed to giving God glory. What can we learn from this? Read Psalm 147 and 150. Have you ever been some place, surrounded by natural beauty, and felt like praising God or singing? Describe it.

3. Was there a time when listening to a worship song brought you out of discouragement? Read Psalm 30:10-11.

YOU ARE BRINGING LIGHT WHERE
DARKNESS HAS REIGNED BEFORE.
THERE WILL BE WARFARE.
COME PREPARED WITH THE
WEAPONS OF PRAISE.

CHAPTER 17

Joy and Gratitude

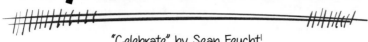

"Celebrate" by Sean Feucht[1]

A River of Joy

He would come by our house and sit down at the upright piano. Soon his hands would be flying over the keys, as he played ragtime music. After he entertained us with tune after tune, he and my Dad would tell funny jokes. I loved what happened next. The man's smile would stretch from ear to ear. He'd place his hands on his mid-section, and start to get giddy. Soon, he'd be laughing so hard that he'd let out little snorts. It was impossible to be in the same room with him and not start laughing yourself.

This man was my Southern Baptist Pastor, Harry Byrd. My whole family absolutely adored him and his family. Observing his life, his joy, and his deep love for Jesus made me adore the Man that he loved the most. By the time I was ten years old, I was ready to surrender my heart to Jesus Christ as my Lord and Savior. A few years later, Mr. Byrd and his family moved to Guatemala, where they remained missionaries for many years. But I would never forget the lasting impression this joyous man had on my life.

In the book "Reckless Devotion," Heidi Baker states, "Cities are reached when we are so full of Jesus' joy that people everywhere are astounded by Him and attracted to Him."[2] The world needs to see ambassadors for Christ with a smile on their faces.

Having joy is crucial in drawing others to hear the message of Christ. It also has a tremendous restorative property that sustains the mission worker through difficult times. Nehemiah 8:10b tells us that *the joy of the Lord will be our strength.* One thing I never knew until years later was that during the years he lived in my hometown, Pastor Byrd had received derogatory statements and anonymous phone calls, threatening him and his family. It was the 1960s and we were living in a small rural town in Virginia. Apparently, some in the community had not liked his messages of love and racial reconciliation. You would have never known he was carrying this weight. His effervescent, joyous demeanor and his love for others were a direct result of his love for his Savior and his rooted identity as a child of God.

> "JOY IS THE INTENSELY PERSONAL EXPERIENCE OF BEING A PARTICIPANT IN THE TRIUMPH OF CHRIST."
> -CHARLES STOCK

Rolland and Heidi Baker, who live and minister in Mozambique, also inspire me with the joy they manifest. They have many responsibilities—many hungry children to feed, many villages to reach with the gospel, churches to oversee, staff issues to resolve, speaking engagements to fulfill, and more. Yet they find ways to go into "the secret place" and become refreshed as they are reminded of God's love and faithfulness. They come out of that place of intimacy and minster with great joy. Rolland writes about this and the role that joy plays in their lives:

> Heidi and I could never have endured this long without a river of life and joy flowing out of our innermost beings. We are not cynical and downcast about the world or the Church, but we are thrilled with our perfect Savior, who is able to finish what He began in us... Joy, laughter, and a light heart are not disrespectful of God and incongruous in this world. Instead, they are evidence of the life of heaven...Joy is not an abstract concept but a tangible

reality. It is birthed in His presence and can fill us, empower us. If you currently struggle to find joy, ask Jesus to fill you afresh.[3]

Charles Stock, also, often seems to have tapped into a river of joy. He writes in his book, *Glow in the Dark*:

> The joy of the Lord gives a great strength. Like agape love, it is sovereign and not subject to external circumstances. Joy overcomes the outward and obvious situation. It sets captives free and can turn victims into more than conquerors. Joy is the intensely personal experience of being a participant in the Triumph of Christ.[4]

No chapter on joy would be complete without mentioning Georgian and Winnie Banov. I introduced them earlier, but this time I want to emphasize that they are sometimes called "joy apostles." To be completely honest, when I first heard them speak at Life Center, I thought to myself, *How can these people be this happy?* Then I attended their ministry school, GCSSM, for two years. As I listened and observed their lives, I learned that their joy was completely genuine. It too, was rooted in their belief in the truths of the finished work of Christ, just as both Charles and Rolland had described. Their lessons on the significance of joy had a profound effect on how I viewed ministry. Unfortunately, my first year at the school happened to be my last year of working at Center for Champions. How I wish I'd heard this message when I first started the program years before.

Paul tells us in Philippians 4:4, *"Always be full of joy in the Lord. I say it again—rejoice!"* Being joyful is a command, just like the commands to love one another or to forgive each other. Remember, God's not going to ask you to do something that you can't do. Not everybody is automatically joyful, but we can learn to be more joyful by finding what helps fuel our joy and identifying what steals it.

What Fuels or Steals Our Joy?

At the school, one of our required readings was a little book called, *Possessing Joy, A Secret to Strength and Longevity* by Steve Backlund. In it, he gives daily teachings relating to joy. You shouldn't be fooled by its seemingly insignificant size. It packs a punch of truth and gives practical ways to become a more expressively joyful person. Backland discusses an important factor that affects the joy of those of us in ministry. God revealed to him that he was being too "harvest focused" and not enough "planting focused." He says:

> Harvest focused people are regularly looking for results and fruit to determine if they are successful or in God's will...Those who base their happiness and joy on visible fruit will not be very joyful, and will have a "roller coaster" emotional experience. "Planting focused" people have established a clear set of core values that they are convinced will bring a great harvest.[5]

When we are "planting focused," we've come to the decision that the results aren't up to us. There will be fruit, even if we don't see it right away, because God asked us to plant. We find joy in remembering what Jesus did for us, His finished work, and being a child of such a good Father. We find joy in loving the ones that God loves so much. *Love doesn't act for results, it just loves.* Our love for Jesus compels us to go. We have an inner sense of joy just knowing that we are doing what our Friend asked us to do. We are planting where He told us to plant. Backland continues:

> If we have a plan from God in planting and watering, we can put up with a lot of lack and unresolved situations. On the contrary, we will be "open season" for the devil if we are using fruit and results as the main indicator of whether we are in God's will or are spiritually "successful." Indeed, our joy is greatly impacted by whether we are harvest focuses or planting focused.[6]

I've been on that roller coaster that Backland was talking about—so happy when some of the inner-city teens made wise choices, and so devastated when they did not. Of course, we all want to see that our efforts are having some type of effect. We just can't let our actions and our emotions be driven by that desire.

I wish I had known just how important it is to pursue and express joy when I was involved in doing compassion ministry. Sometimes, the stories of the people's lives are so disheartening, and your resources to meet their needs seem limited. Day-by-day sowing into the lives of children and their families takes time to see fruit, and can feel draining. It's not unusual for missionaries and social workers to feel beaten down and emotionally depleted. But living in a state of depletion is not what God wants for us and it doesn't help those we are called to serve. God wants to renew us with His unconditional love and overflowing joy, so that we operate out of that which never runs dry.

During the years at the Center, each of us would try to find ways to renew our joy. First, we would seek a renewal of joy in our personal devotions, and second, in times together as a team of staff and volunteers. Often, before the kids would come, we'd play worship music, sing, and soak in the truths about God's goodness and what He'd done in our lives. We would find joy when we could.

Many days, some of us would be joking around with the little kids or the teens. At the end of the day, sometimes the staff would meet to debrief. Certainly, we'd discuss some of the difficult things that may have happened. But occasionally we'd talk about some of the good things, and even the funny things the little kids or the teens said or did.

On a few rare occasions, our staff got just plain silly. One time, it was the end of a busy week in the after-school program. We were cleaning up the kitchen at the church where we met. There were bags of stale bread on the counter. Someone from Panera would get bread and give it to the church and to the Center. We gave away as much as people wanted but there were still a few old stale rolls and baguettes sitting around that no one wanted. I was about to throw out a crusty roll, when one of the staff said something to me in a teasing way. I don't know what came over me, but all of a sudden, I saw this roll flying through the air, hitting my coworker. Well, not to be outdone, she threw it back at me. Other staff joined in the bread throwing fight. Then I noticed the baguettes. *Hmm. Reminds me of a baseball bat!* Next thing I know, we were playing stale roll baseball. The fun and laughter washed away some of the struggles from the past week. It helped to refresh us.

Walking in Gratitude

A tremendous way to have more joy is to rehearse the wonderful things that God has done in your life and to endeavor to live from a place of gratitude. As we talk about increasing joy in our lives, one of the best ways, in my opinion, is to stop thinking about the things we wish we had, and instead start to focus on all the things for which we can be thankful.

Often, when I walked into our program, which was located in a beautiful old church building that once held 1000 members, I'd thank God that this place was available for us to use at such a reasonable cost. Yes, it was located on one of the worst crime ridden streets, but that's where the families we wanted to reach lived. Yes, the kitchen flooded at times and there was always some evidence of mice, but *hey*, we were thankful that we had a large full kitchen where we could have our monthly family dinners. We could, and did, serve as many as eighty to ninety people, counting parents and children in attendance. Occasionally we had no heat, but we made do with space heaters and warm coats, or maybe even took a day off for everybody. I was thankful that when we had art class we didn't have to worry about ruining new furniture or carpet, as there was none.

In the beginning years, I noticed the needs and the lack more than the things for which to be thankful. When I needed more staff and helpers, I'd be discouraged and even a little frustrated when an intern or staff person left after only a short while. Once, while attending Holy Given Ministry School, I asked Lesley Anne Leighton how she handled having interns come and go.

She said, "Like this!" and held the palms of her hands wide open.

Her words and her demonstrative gesture helped me start to be much more grateful for any amount of time a volunteer, intern, or staff member could give to our ministry. Not everyone is called to stay at the ministry that God has called you to. You may be called to stay a long time. They may have been called for only a season. However, their time serving in the ministry, even if it appears short, can prove to be extremely helpful. So be grateful for all the wonderful people that God allows you to know and serve with, no matter the length of time.

The Benefits of Gratitude

Gratitude is a big part of refreshing your heart and soul, and increasing your joy. One Sunday, Pastor Charles talked about the benefits of gratitude. In his sermon, he referred to some articles that he had read about the impact of gratitude on one's life. Inspired, I did a little searching and found an interesting article, which may have been the one he was quoting. In *Psychology Today,* Amy Morin listed seven specific benefits to having gratitude:

Gratitude opens the doors to more relationships (and also better ones).

- Gratitude improves physical health.

- Gratitude improves psychological health.

- Gratitude enhances empathy **and reduces aggression.**

- Grateful people sleep **better.**

- Gratitude improves self-esteem.

- Gratitude increases mental strength.[7]

1 Thessalonians 5:16-18 says, *"Always be joyful. Never stop praying. Be thankful in all circumstances, for this is God's will for you who belong to Christ Jesus."*

There are so many gifts to be grateful for when you are doing ministry. Take time to stop and notice them. Be grateful that you have something to give and others who are helping you. At Life Center our motto is, "Experiencing the love of God and giving it away!" There is so much joy in giving. We get blessed by serving those in need. Joy comes from seeing lives changed. It comes from knowing you answered God's call. If we focus on all these things, our joy will be full.

Reflection and Action

LISTEN

- "Celebrate" by Sean Feucht

STUDY

- Read Philippians 1:1-9 and Psalm 103. Then do a topical Bible search on joy and write down the verses that speak to you.

JOURNAL

1. Do you consider yourself a joyful person or do you struggle to be joyful on a consistent basis?

2. If you struggle to be joyful, consider what may be stealing your joy and also what brings you joy. How can you change your life to stay in the joyful place?

3. Make a list of things you are grateful for. Consider starting a weekly thankfulness journal, especially if you need a boost of joy and gratitude.

CHAPTER 18

The Secret Places

"So Will I (100 Billion X)" by Hillsong United[1]

Jesus Communed with His Father

The gospel of Mark starts off with a bang! There are no stories of shepherds in the field waiting for a Messiah, no twelve-year-old boy in the temple speaking with the elders, no poetic description of Jesus being the Word and the Word being flesh, no dreams, and no long genealogies. Right away Mark tells us of Jesus getting baptized, being tempted for 40 days, and starting to minister to people. We read of many people getting healed, demons cast out, and Peter's mother-in-law's fever getting healed, *immediately.* She felt so well that she got up and even prepared dinner for the disciples. All this, and more, happens in the first chapter.

Mark's gospel speaks of a Person that the local people crowded around the door to see heal the sick. He did not disappoint. Some commentaries refer to the book of Mark as the gospel in a *hurry.* The word "immediately" is used numerous times. But right smack in the middle of this whirlwind of activity in Peter's hometown are these verses:

> *Before daybreak the next morning, Jesus got up and went out to an isolated place to pray. Later Simon and the others went out to find him. When they found him, they said, "Everyone is looking for you." But Jesus replied, "We must go on to the other towns as well, and I will preach to them, too. That is why I came* (Mark 1:35-38).

Let's consider the scenario. The morning after all the people had been at Peter's house, there was a crowd of people who were waiting to see

Jesus again. The disciples wake up, and Jesus is nowhere to be found. Peter and the others go looking for Him. When Peter finally finds Jesus in some isolated place, one might wonder if his words don't come with a slight edge when he says, *"Everyone is looking for you"* (Mark 1:37b).

Peter seems to be implying something like this, "Man, Jesus, where have you been? We've been looking all over for you. Don't you realize all these people are waiting for you? What are you doing?"

Peter most likely knew these people who were waiting to see more of "this miracle man." Jesus' response was unexpected. He didn't go back down to Peter's house to continue where He left off, even though His ministry there had been quite successful. Why not? He took some private, quiet time with His Father, where He could actually hear and focus on what the Father was saying. During this time in the secret place of fellowship with His Father, God confirmed that He was asking Jesus to go on to other towns. Also, it was in that place of rest and attentiveness to the Father's voice, that He had His purpose reaffirmed, *"That is why I came"* (Mark 1:38). The time with His Father gave Jesus the strength to do only what God was asking Him to do, and in this case, resist the pull of obligation to His friends and the crowds of needy people looking for Him.

When you get involved in ministry work, things can get extremely busy quickly. There is a world of needy people, and knowing just one often opens a door to meeting many more. I learned the hard way that it was easy to get distracted from my main purpose. Without intentional times to regroup, a minister can run from one urgent situation to another, never stopping to catch their breath and be renewed in God's presence. The demand of needs starts to shift our focus off our trust that God has a plan and a specific purpose for us. Without time to reflect, we forget to embrace the fact that we are not responsible for everybody's problems. This mistake is a major contributor to ministry burnout.

What was it that helped Jesus set the pace of His ministry? What guided Him as to when, where, and how to minister? John 5:19 gives a significant clue into how Jesus operated, *"So Jesus explained, 'I tell you the truth, the Son can do nothing by himself. He does only what he sees the Father doing. Whatever the Father does, the Son also does.'"*

An important key in doing ministry well is to do what you sense the Father is doing. How do we know where He is leading? How do we see more clearly? We must follow Jesus' example and find a secret place to be with God where we can be alone to focus on His Word and hear His voice. Spending time in the secret place helps to prepare our hearts and minds to pray and hear from God. Then, as we are out and about, walking in communion with God, we can start silently having a conversation, asking Him to show us who needs ministry. When I've decided to purposely look for opportunities to love like Jesus, I've had some wonderfully encouraging encounters with total strangers. The joy on their faces when I've shared the Father's heart for them, in turn, has refreshed and renewed my soul.

> AN IMPORTANT KEY IN DOING MINISTRY WELL IS TO DO WHAT YOU SENSE THE FATHER IS DOING.

One time during His ministry, Jesus had just been told that John the Baptist had been beheaded. He wanted to be alone to grieve the loss of this godly man, who was also a close relative. So he got into a boat and went to the other side of the lake, but as soon as he landed there was a huge crowd of people waiting for him. His compassion compelled him to stay and pray for them. (Matthew 14:13-14)

In this case, when Jesus really needed some time apart, His heart of compassion caused Him to forego His alone time with God. Instead, He reached out to the crowd, teaching, healing and multiplying food to thousands. As He was dwelling in communion with God, He must have seen that this was what the Father was doing at that particular time. It was quite a long day. At the end of it, Jesus sent the disciples away in a boat, and He finally got to take that time to be alone with God. Mathew 14:23 states, *"After sending them home, he went up into the hills by himself to pray. Night fell while he was there alone."*

A significant aspect of the secret place is this state of being in communion with God. Psalm 91:1 says, *"He who dwells in the secret place of the Most High, shall abide under the shadow of the Almighty"* (NKJV). The verse isn't speaking about dwelling or living in a place alone, away from everybody. It's talking about a state of dwelling—with God in our heart and mind—in constant communion. You can be in that communion even as you are addressing the needs of others. The key is to live in communion with God so that you can know when is the right time to get away to renew and when is the right time to stay and be involved in what you sense God is doing at that moment.

There are numerous scriptures telling us of Jesus getting alone to speak with His Father. However, as we see in Matthew 14, sometimes even He had to postpone His alone time with God. But He didn't let the needs of others deter Him from later getting away to process and commune with His Father. I know ministry leaders who diligently take an hour every day to pray, read the Bible, and/or listen to worship music. The important thing is to remember you are in the secret place to spend time with the Father, to dwell, not just to check off a religious list of daily disciplines.

One leader told me that he also sets aside an entire eight-hour day every month to renew and hear what God is saying for his life and his ministry. That's such a great idea, if one can possibly manage to do this. Heidi Baker is known to spend significant time "soaking" in God's presence, even though many people are waiting for her to discuss some of the needs of her ministry. She has made it a priority to have intimate times to "press in," as she calls it, and encounter God, so she can come out of that place full and ready to pour out.

Some Have to Contend for Secret Places

We are all wired differently. For some, finding that quiet place and blocking out distractions can be difficult. I'll be honest. I deal with some type of ADD, and sitting quietly for an hour doing a devotional or soaking in God's presence is very hard for me unless I remove myself from many of the things that vie for my attention. If you are easily distracted, like I am, you may need "to contend" to find these undistracted times. It takes real effort, but it's worth it. As shown in Mark 1, even Jesus removed Himself from the house where many people were sleeping and went up to the mountain to pray. I like to go outside and sit in a quiet place on my deck, or if possible, go away to a special location. If I'm sitting in a cluttered, busy room in my house, with my cell phone nearby, I easily get off track.

Once, I was determined to have a quiet time and read the Bible. I even set the timer on my cell phone for one hour to help me keep to my goal. It was Christmas time and I chose to sit across from the nicely decorated Christmas tree. Soon my mind drifted to a picture I had taken of my cute grandkids in front of the tree. I then found myself posting the picture on Facebook. One thing led to another, and soon I was lost in the world of social media until my focus was jarred by the beeping of the phone alarm. *Oh, my goodness, an hour is up already.* I remembered why I was sitting there holding the Bible. I shook my head and thought to myself, *Pitiful.*

But, guess what? God knows how I am and He loves me anyway. I've had to learn and accept this. If you are like me and struggle to be disciplined, don't beat yourself up. Keep trying and keep looking for what works for you. You will find it. Disciplined and organized people are so wonderfully amazing to me; but I can start to feel very bad about myself, when I consider that, even at my age, I have never mastered the art of daily devotions or regular long soaking times. Getting down on myself about this, however, doesn't bring me into deeper times with God. It just exacerbates the situation. As I've said before, this book is not for the ones who have it all together—it's for the many of us who greatly desire to be used by God, yet often struggle at doing the things that we know a "good believer" *should* do.

So, here's a little advice for people who are more like I am. Just because you get distracted, don't give up. Maybe set smaller goals—like fifteen or thirty minutes to sit down with your Bible or to pray, not one long hour. It may take you a little more planning and effort to find those special quiet times to be alone with God and read your Bible. The effort pays off.

Remembering how valuable God's life-giving Word is, and how it gives you a foundation for all you do and say, will help motivate you to make time to read it. No spiritual book, or even a song, can replace the living Word of God. As we read the gospels and see how Jesus treated others, our desire to help the hurting increases. As we study sections of the epistles, such as Romans 6, 7, and 8, we are reminded of who we are in Christ. As we are filled with the life-giving message of the love of God, then we have something to give away.

You can also saturate your environment with His presence by listening to the Bible, podcast teachings, or worship music while going about your daily tasks. "Secret places" may be found in the most unlikely settings. God sometimes speaks to me in the middle of a thousand people at a worship service at my church. He might speak to you through a song, a sunset, a phone call, a picture on the refrigerator, or even an article or a picture of a friend on Facebook.

I can get completely immersed in God's presence while driving alone in my car, especially if I'm going a long distance. I turn the key and start listening to my Pandora worship station. In a short time, I'm talking to Jesus and singing His praises. One year, I had to drive four hours to Virginia and four hours back every month, as I cared for my elderly mother. Although my mother's sickness and needs were so disheartening, I found my time in the car to be a sanctuary.

Once I was driving on Harrisburg inner-city streets and a worship song came on the radio that described "roaring over the city." I started belting out that song, and didn't see the speed limit changed from 50 to 35. Alas, the cop didn't appear to be one who would accept any excuses. He was all business, "Ma'am, can I see your registration…." He showed no signs of mercy. So, if you choose driving as one of your "secret places," be careful, it could cost you.

Nature's Renewing Powers

A great way to prevent burnout is to seek the secret places that can be found in nature. So much about nature seems to draw our focus to God. Many of Jesus' secret places were out in natural settings—mountains, lakes, and gardens. David describes the natural world in numerous memorable psalms. He speaks of things like the heavens, the stars, the moon, the waves, the mountain stream, the lightning, and the thunder clap. Sometimes, just being out in God's creation, enjoying His handiwork, can be a type of communion. As the psalmist said, *"He makes me to lie down in green pastures; He leads me beside the still waters. He restores my soul"* (Ps. 23:2-3a NKJV).

I've previously shared my love of everything that involves an ocean setting—the sea oats waving in the gentle breeze, the smell of the salty air, and the sun glistening on the water. Sometimes, as I stand in front of that great ocean expanse, I can't help but burst out into singing, knowing that the crashing roar of the waves will drown out the sound, because my song is meant to be shared with only One.

Some people love a strenuous hike in the mountains, straining to get to the top peak of some amazing summit that looks down over miles and miles of green valleys and a river below in the distance. Others might enjoy a jog down a country road, along acres of fences, past the Holsteins and the silos, fields of corn stalks bulging with fresh tasseled corn, ready to be picked. In the movie, *Chariots of Fire*, Eric Liddell, the famous Olympic runner, who later became a missionary to China, made this statement, "I believe God made me for a purpose, but He also made me fast. And when I run, I feel His pleasure."[2] I believe that when we are able to go out into the beautiful places of God's creation, we feel His pleasure. It's not a waste of time to indulge your senses with all the beauty that God created. Let yourself be in the moment. Breath in and then let it out. It's absolutely essential to renew your mind, body, and spirit if you want to keep running your race for God.

Of course, not everyone has the time or opportunity to be around natural beauty on a regular basis. Fortunately, God encounters and quiet times can happen in all kinds of places. There are those who find a way to renew without going anywhere special. Busy moms may find it inspiring to hear how John Wesley's mother, Susanna, who had 10 (living) children, would sit in a chair and pull her apron over her head and pray. When she did that, the children knew to let mother have her alone time with God.[3] It's true that our God is a personal God—He speaks to each of us uniquely. If your heart is to spend some alone time to be with God, it really doesn't matter the setting, He's just glad you came.

In summary, if you want to be useful to God and be able to stay in the race for some length of time, you *need* to find ways to renew your soul. It's true that it is not always easy to do. Even disciplined people are sometimes distracted. But it is so worth pressing in and finding a way. Look for God encounters and purposefully set aside time to focus on God to hear what He is saying. God is waiting to meet with you and whisper secrets to your heart. The next step is up to you. Cherish and make time for the secret places.

Reflection and Action

LISTEN

- "So Will I (100 Billion X)" by Hillsong United

STUDY

- Luke 9:18, Luke 22:39, Psalm 46:10, Psalm 91:1, Psalm 29:1-11, Psalm 19:1-6, Psalm 139:1-18

JOURNAL

1. How do you regularly make time to be alone with God and what does that look like?

2. Describe a special encounter with God that stands out to you; either while in a private secret place or going about life, walking in communion with God.

3. Where are some of your favorite "secret places" with God?

IF YOU WANT TO BE USEFUL TO GOD AND BE ABLE TO STAY IN THE RACE FOR SOME LENGTH OF TIME, YOU NEED TO FIND WAYS TO RENEW YOUR SOUL.

CHAPTER 19

The Beautiful Body of Christ

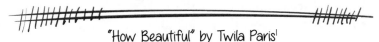

"How Beautiful" by Twila Paris[1]

Enveloped in Liquid Love

It was another one of those difficult weeks. Hurtful words had been thrown my way, and that ever present, nagging feeling of inadequacy as a leader encompassed my thoughts. Physically I was exhausted. Late night hours and stress have a way of wearing you out. That Wednesday, I dragged myself into the evening service at my church.

Our church had recently moved to a new building. The room in which we were temporarily meeting before our sanctuary was built had a low ceiling, poles that blocked the view of the stage, and areas with dim lighting. I chose to sit in one of those dimly lit sections that night. I didn't want to participate. I just wanted to "soak" and renew. I stretched out my whole body across three chairs, leaning back and taking a moment to catch my breath and absorb the manifest presence of God, which I could almost always sense hovering in the room during services.

There was supposed to be a speaker that night, but at the last minute he was unable to come. Pastor Charles announced that we were turning the night into a soaking worship evening. Yay, I had come to the right service! Soft music played from skilled hands, scriptures were read, and spontaneous moments of songs in worship gently flowed over the audio system. I loved soaking nights. I really needed this. *Why didn't I stop and do this at home more often?*

Then Charles came to the mic and said he felt that we were to bless and pray for certain people that night. He started to name the ones he wanted to come down to the front of the stage. One was a man who spent the weekend night hours giving out food and clothing to the homeless. Then two couples were called. One of the couples had chosen to travel to many locations in the US with their three children, doing puppet shows for children in the public schools and at community fairs, sharing the love of God through the arts. And lastly, he said my name and talked about the ministry of Center for Champions to the inner-city families. Quite surprised, I lifted myself off the chairs and knelt down beside these amazing people who loved the lost and the needy, people I admired so much.

Then Charles read scriptures including, "*Whoever is kind to the poor lends to the Lord. And he will reward them for what they have done*" (Prov. 19:17, NIV). And a verse about the fatherless, "*A father to the fatherless, a defender of widows, is God in his holy habitation*" (Ps. 68:5, NKJV). Next, he asked people in the congregation who felt led to pray for us to come forward. They stood around, gently laid hands on us, and quietly or silently prayed. I don't remember if anyone had a prophetic word for me that night. I just remember the prophetic act that followed.

Charles opened a bottle of oil that was on the stage, and proceeded to anoint our heads. But this was no typical drop of oil placed gently on the forehead. This was him lifting the bottle and pouring out the oil on the top of our heads until it ran down the sides of our faces. In that moment, it felt like the touch of a thousand hands, believers standing with me in a show of support and appreciation. The oil felt hot and soothing, and I was enveloped in what I can only best describe as "liquid love."

For years, I had known this scripture, "*Behold how good and pleasant it is for brethren to dwell together in unity*" (Ps. 133:1, NKJV). But I never really thought much at all about the next verse, "*It is like the precious oil upon the head, running down on the beard, the beard of Aaron, running down on the edge of his garments"* (Ps. 133:2, NKJV).

That night, I experienced what it was like to be supported and loved by the beautiful Body of Christ. Even as I write this, I swallow hard, and my mind takes me back to that euphoric moment. I venture to say that this unique experience of feeling so cherished by the members of my church and my pastor, along with the act of kneeling with comrades of like-heart for the lost and needy, kept me in the race for many years to come.

Family and Ministry

Another thing that helped me keep on running with the vision that God had given me was the support of my family. My husband was first and foremost the greatest help to me, and to the ministry God was calling me to. He never complained when he had to make his own supper, night after night, while I drove children home or closed up the Center on weeknights. (Fortunately, my sons were off to college by then). He cheerfully and generously supported the ministry with his finances. He listened and offered encouragement when things felt overwhelming or I needed godly advice. And, he essentially gave me away for large segments of time. He's also been my encourager and first editor as I write this book. I'm not proud to say it, but I'm pretty sure I neglected him way too much. I don't recommend *that.* (He read this and wanted me to tell you that he didn't feel neglected and that this was his contribution to the ministry. OK, true, but I *do feel like I* neglected him.)

I was fortunate to have the support of my husband. If you're married, it's crucial to have this support. It's not necessary that both spouses work together in ministry, but they do need to agree on the value of the mission and support the decision of the one who is involved. It can make the difference in whether you finish the race God called you to run or whether you give up too soon.

It's important to remember that while you are helping the hurting, you also need to be aware of the concerns of your own family. Isaiah 58 talks about the kind of fast that God wants from us. *"What I'm interested in seeing you do is: sharing your food with the hungry, inviting the homeless poor into your homes, putting clothes on the shivering ill-clad, **being available to your own families***" (Isaiah 58: 7, MSG, emphasis mine)

Caring for your children and your spouse is ministry, also. The greatest ministry I ever had was being mother to my two sons; teaching them, praying for them and dreaming that they would grow up and influence the world with God's love. And they did! Keep Jesus' love and words at the center of your relationships and let that overflow to both the ones you serve in ministry and to those in your family. You might not always be able to measure it in equal amounts of time spent, but keep your family in your heart and focus.

If you have a younger family with children still at home, you will need to be especially vigilant about making time for your spouse and children. When you are able to be with them, be *present*—focus, listen, play, and have fun. The needs of the world and the needy people you serve will always be pulling on your time, but you can't let it pull you away from giving unconditional love to your spouse and children. If possible, find ways to include them in your ministry and make it a part of what defines your family. ***Find time and focus for family.***

Find Your People

Too often, we talk about the problems in the body of Christ, while seldom emphasizing what a gift we are to one another. A coal burning alone will soon go out, therefore not using all of its full potential. However, coals stacked next to one another burn brighter and longer, providing warmth and light for those nearby. Put yourself next to "the burning ones"—those passionately in love with God and passionately in love with the ones that God has put on their heart. ***Find your people.***

To be successful, you will need others who believe in your ministry and lend support. There were those who believed passionately in our urban ministry. Some generously supported us financially, and came to our rescue time and again. Some fervently prayed for our concerns when contacted or led by the Lord. When you step out and decide to minister to others, you will *need* praying intercessors.

Let me put this another way. If you come with the love of God, bringing practical help, and giving freedom to those held captive by Satan and his hellish ways, you will need prayer warriors fighting on your behalf. They will be the ones standing with you, calling down strongholds and praying for the powers of heaven to protect, sustain, and guide you. Even people you don't know that well, like unassuming, wonderful grandmothers in your church, can be some of your greatest prayer helpers. ***Find some warriors.***

As I was writing this book, I went through some old files. I found some copies of the emails I sent to a few close friends in those early years of starting Center for Champions. I was embarrassed as I read through a few of them because they were three pages long! It was twenty years ago—I guess I considered emails to be like letters in those days. They were long because I wanted, and possibly needed, to share my dreams for the ministry with my friends. I also needed to vent my concerns to somebody besides my poor husband, who had heard it all. What amazed me the most was that these friends wrote back. And it certainly appeared from their responses that they had actually read what I had written.

These were busy women. Some had professional, high pressure jobs. One pastored a large church. She could have easily just not responded. I would have gotten the message that she didn't have the time to read my updates. But that didn't happen. Once when I apologized to these friends for my long emails, this pastor responded that perhaps this was my way of processing all that was going on. Her response was so freeing. It helped me not feel so stupid, and gave a reason for my writing. She's also encouraged me to write this book.

If you choose to go into some kind of ministry, surround yourself with a few good friends who have your back, friends who will listen to your rants with empathy, giving suggestions full of God's wisdom. Your friends also need to be those who love you enough to tell you what you need to hear, not just what you want to hear. Proverbs 27:17 certainly applies here, *"As iron sharpens iron, so a friend sharpens a friend."* Reach out to those who share your vision for helping others and who love you unconditionally. It's so precious when we find a few of these relationships. ***Cherish dear friends.***

We were never meant to do ministry alone. Jesus sent His disciples out two by two. Paul continually paired with various people in his stressful, challenging ministry. There was Paul and Barnabus, Paul and Silas, Paul and Luke, and then, Paul with the young man he referred to as a dear son in the faith, Timothy. At other times, we see his endearing love and joy expressed for a whole community of believers, such as those from Philippi.

I'm so thankful for those who labored with me the longest at Center for Champions: *Linda, Eric, Tara, and Richie,* just to name a few. And I'm thankful for those who could only give us one year or even one semester. Bonnie Lonski was my co-founder, who could only stay a few months once our program began, but her "Can Do" spirit helped to balance my lack of confidence. I'm sure God brought her into my life to help me gets this ministry off the ground.

The people you minister with may become some of your closest friends. Together you receive encouragement, understanding, assistance, prayer, kindness, and joy. Together you accomplish so much more for the kingdom than you could ever accomplish alone. Heidi Baker describes the great value of the body of Christ:

> The Body of Christ is such an amazing thing. In it God brings together diverse people with diverse gifts who can work together to accomplish His purposes. It is a sign and a wonder to our world

when the Body functions and the seemingly impossible is achieved through the cooperation and commitment to a common goal. [2]

I can't say it any better than that. Some of your greatest treasures will be found in the Body of Christ.

Reflection and Action

LISTEN

- *"How Beautiful"* by Twila Paris

- This song is from the 90s but the melody is still beautifully sung and the words are so true.

STUDY

- Read these scriptures in both *The Message* and the *New Living Translation*: Philippians 1:1-11, 2: 19-30, and Philippians 4:1, 2 Timothy 1:1-9.

JOURNAL

1. Do you have a group of people who are prayer intercessors for your life and ministry? If not make a list and contact them soon.

2. When you are with your family are you really *present*—involved, listening, and relating? Are there ways you can involve your family in your ministry?

3. Do you have a few dear friends who you can call day or night that will be with you in the good and bad times of your life? Call, text, or write them an appreciative email very soon, when you are not in need.

REACH OUT TO THOSE WHO
SHARE YOUR VISION FOR
HELPING OTHERS AND WHO
LOVE YOU UNCONDITIONALLY.

Crossing the Finish Line

CHAPTER 20

Success, Failure, and Rewards

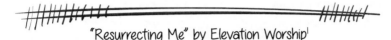

"Resurrecting Me" by Elevation Worship[1]

The Joy of Changed Lives

It was a pleasant May afternoon when we gathered at a community park for our Center for Champions end-of-the-school-year picnic. All the kids were there—children, teens, and even some CFC program graduates—along with some of their parents. It would be my last picnic as executive director and even as a board member. It was time for me to totally pass the baton to the next generation of staff and volunteers. Linda, my dear, dear friend and comrade, the one who had stuck with me and the Center for 15 years, had planned a special goodbye.

She lined up several of the program students, ages ranging from 6-22 years old. One by one they came up to the mic and shared what Center for Champions had meant to their lives. Of course, the oldest ones touched my heart most deeply, because I knew their stories and could see the transformation in their lives.

There was Natalie, all grown up, an attractive young woman who had graduated from high school. She was now working in a job as a security officer at a prestigious hotel. When we first met her, she was a shy little seven-year-old girl. Academics were a struggle for her at times, but in dance she shined. Natalie was so gifted that she was added to the dance team at a much younger age than most. When she was fourteen, CFC took a small group of students to Haiti on a mission trip. There, she taught the island children a few dances and ministered at a local church service. That trip helped to change her quiet and reserved identity to one of poise and confidence. Now, here she was years later, still making time to come by the Center to lead our younger girls in the dance program. I was so proud of this young lady as I listened to her share how much the Center had meant to her.

Then there was Sean. Remember him? He's the boy in the chapter on fatherlessness who asked Jesus into his heart when he was seven years old. He was now sixteen, still coming to the Center, now faithfully attending the teen group meetings. He took the mic and shared how the Center had helped his life and helped him to know God. Tears welled up in my eyes as he and the others shared. Lastly, one of the moms spoke of the many ways the Center had changed her life and the lives of her children. Then, she gave me one of her big bear hugs. I was becoming completely undone, in a good way.

After everyone had finished sharing, Linda handed me a pretend torch, which was so appropriate. I passed the torch symbolically to Jeff, the new executive director. That day, seeing what the Center meant to the families, hearing the new children talk about how much they loved coming there, and observing how some of our graduates had defied the odds of their community and were now living happy and productive lives, was part of my reward for answering God's call to start the Center for Champions. That day, I was so glad that I had stayed, instead of quitting eight years earlier. Just one day like that last day made hundreds of tough afternoons at the Center pale in comparison.

My desire in writing this book has been to help turn your feelings of compassion for the downtrodden into some type of consistent loving action. I'm not telling my stories so you'll think what a good program Center for Champions has been. I tell them to paint pictures, with the hope that they will help you start to visualize yourself doing something that makes a positive, lasting difference in another human being's life.

Action takes motivation. The fundamental reasons to serve those in need are our love for Jesus and His love for others. That in itself is enough. There is the reality, however, that helping the oppressed, the fatherless, and the ones just needing someone to give them a helping hand, comes with *an indescribable joy*. These opportunities can be so rewarding and give you a unique feeling of purposeful living. And while the reward of a job well done is not our reason for serving, it is great motivation.

Changing the Inner City for Christ, One Family at a Time

For many years, CFC's motto was: *Changing the Inner City for Christ, One Family at a Time*. We knew we couldn't reach every family in our city, but at least we could reach those that crossed our path. We saw parents become more involved in their children's lives at the Center and at their schools. Consistently, 75% of the parents attended our monthly parent dinners. Many of the parents accepted Jesus Christ as Lord of their lives and sought to make changes in their homes. The teens who came to our program graduated from high school, some becoming the first in their family to graduate. Normally this would not be considered that significant of an achievement, however, the Harrisburg School District had a *graduation rate in the 2012-2013 school year of only 38%*. The lowest in the state.[2] A few of the parents even chose to get married in a community where marriage is not the norm. Seeing the fruit of our investment in the lives of individual families was wonderfully rewarding.

One family whose lives were positively changed by our intervention recently came to my attention. I saw a Facebook update from a young lady who had been part of CFC. In the picture, she and her bridegroom were decked out in elegant clothing, adorned with royal elements, such as crowns and robes that are part of the Orthodox Coptic Christian Church wedding ceremonial proceedings.

A year earlier I'd seen her post about graduating from college. I made arrangements to meet her for a congratulatory dinner. That night she told me that she had been accepted into graduate school. How the years had gone by! And now she was so accomplished, so confident, and on the road to success and the pursuit of happiness here in her adopted country. My heart swelled with thankfulness as I remembered the first time I had met this girl and her brother.

One day many years before, two children appeared at the steps of CFC. They spoke very little English. We sent them home with application papers and a note saying that someone had to fill them out. They returned the next day with completed applications, and soon became immersed in all the activities we had to offer.

The young girl, who was about eleven years of age and a couple of years older than her brother, knew a little bit of English. Since they had just arrived from Egypt, her brother only knew their native language of Arabic. We enlisted this bright young girl's help to interpret some of the homework assignments that he would bring with him. One day, she showed me the tiny cross tattooed on the inside of her wrist that identified her as a Coptic Christian. In her home country, many of her faith had endured extreme persecution. For years my husband and I had supported ministries helping persecuted Christians and now I felt so honored to be able to help a family right here in America.

The children's parents faithfully attended our family dinners. I remember, so clearly, what happened at one of the first group meetings they attended. It was during the Easter season, and I was discussing what Jesus had done for us on the cross and the power of His resurrection. The father's face broke into a huge grin.

"Jesus!" He said, part question and part exclamation. "You teach Jesus?!"

I assured him that we most certainly did teach about Jesus and loved Him very much. He did not realize that Center for Champions was a Christian program. He only knew we were helping his kids learn English. God had divinely directed their steps to the right door. He clapped his hands holding them up to his heart, grinning with a light in his eyes, expressing a type of inner joy that I feel may only be experienced by those believers, those *lovers of Jesus* who have endured trials and persecution. Then he simply said, in the few English words he knew, "Jesus is good!"

The parents were extremely appreciative every time we got involved to help them through some difficult situation. Sadly, on the street and in school, these foreign children met intense bullying. They spoke Arabic, looked Arabic, and this was just a few years after 9/11. Someone almost broke the son's arm at school and the daughter was being called names and attacked by other girls in her school. One day, we got a call that she was being held after school for detention because of getting into a fight. The staff and I were alarmed for her, as we knew that fighting was not her normal character. We were sure that she was only involved in a fight out of self-defense. We didn't want to see this sweet, vulnerable young girl get hurt or start to develop a hardened, tough attitude. We determined to find a better school situation for her and her brother, if possible.

Fortunately, we were able to get both of them into Harrisburg Christian School, with full scholarships. We promised the school's board that CFC would assist throughout the process of adjusting to the new school and with any future issues. Our staff attended special meetings with the family and teachers over a period of several years. Since the girl was heading into middle school, we found an outside tutor to assist her. CFC, along with dedicated teachers in the school, was able to help them succeed in that setting.

As I continued to look at this young lady's pictures posted on Facebook, I saw some that included her brothers and her parents. Seeing the pride and joy on her parents' faces as they stood beside their firstborn, their very accomplished daughter, now married to a young man who shared their same Coptic Christian faith and Egyptian culture, was incredibly encouraging and satisfying. Of course, her own aptitude, determination, and family values contributed enormously to her success, but I also knew that CFC had played a significant part in helping her and the whole family to start, and remain, on a successful path here in our country.

> ...THE INNER JOY AND CONTENTMENT OF KNOWING YOU HELPED TO CHANGE SOMEONE'S LIFE FOR THE BETTER.

I thank God for the beautiful opportunity we were given to help this precious family, when they came as foreigners from another land. Presently there are over 60 million, refugees, or displaced people, around the world.[3.] God tells us to care for the widows, the fatherless, the poor and the foreigner (Zech. 7:9-10). These families are in dire need of practical help, encouragement, and hope. They need to be loved as Jesus would love them. Maybe they will meet Him in your eyes, with your hands, and with your care and concern. Maybe God will call you to be one of the ones to help them, either here in the USA or somewhere else in the world. What a joy it is to be used by God to share His love with some of the ones who need it so desperately.

The *Joy* of Helping is a Reward

How does one put that feeling of knowing you helped somebody into words? That feeling is what I call a *reward*. The word "reward" itself sounds so impotent. It doesn't begin to describe the inner joy and contentment of knowing you helped to change someone's life for the better. It makes answering God's call and staying in the race, despite some disappointments and some times of hardship, worth every minute. It's really a gift from God when you're given the chance to see the effects of your labor in ministry. Some results you may never be able to know in your life time.

The Discouragement of Failure

When doing ministry, there will be those times that appear to be a "success." And then there will also be a number of situations that appear to be "failures." Randy Clark has an informative and encouraging audio teaching and booklet called *The Thrill of Victory/ the Agony of Defeat*.[4] I highly recommend listening to or reading his message. It's helpful to hear from someone who has seen so many people healed share the fact that not everyone he has prayed for has gotten healed. He describes how it feels to face defeat in ministry. His message helps us understand and perhaps accept that everyone faces times when things don't turn out as hoped.

Center for Champions was no exception. I've shared some of the good things that happened from our years of doing inner city ministry, but I also need to be honest about the fact that there were times when things didn't turn out as we had hoped. I have mentioned before that we shouldn't be *too* "harvest focused." Too much focus on how many people's lives we've changed can steal your joy. It did that for me on several occasions, including the day I went to prison to visit some of our former students.

Two teenage boys, who had been in our program for several years before they turned thirteen, had gotten into some serious trouble with stealing. One of them had a horrendous family life situation. But the other one, at least, had a relationship with his father and did well in school. One school year, we made him a junior leader in the after-school program. But when he seemed to enjoy bossing his fellow students around a little too much, I had to remind him of "servant leadership." I was so sure he would beat the odds—go to college, get a good job, and get away from the problems of the inner city.

I was shocked when I heard that these two teens were in the adult county prison. As a clergy person, I was allowed to go inside to visit and sit down and talk with them. This was my first time going into a prison. I was so discouraged knowing that I was going to visit students who had been in our program. The whole process was cold and intimidating, the guards were unsmiling, and there was no lighthearted chatter. It's serious business, as you sign your name and empty your pockets. Once I got the clearance to walk through, *CLANG* the big metal doors slammed behind me.

My heart sank when each young man, dressed in an orange prison jumpsuit, walked down the dark, dull, hallway to the room where I was allowed to meet with them separately. I had not seen them in a few years, and now, as I reached out to hug them, they were towering over me. I gave them my best, "God is with you," talk and tried to understand a little more about the circumstances that had put them there.

As I left and walked out into the blinding sunshine, I rushed to my car to be alone. I opened the door, jumped inside, and quickly placed my hands over my face and leaned my head against the steering wheel. Deep, gut-wrenching sobs poured out of my heart to my Jesus. *Oh Lord, what did we do wrong?* I cried. *Why didn't we have a better influence on these boys? How could they be in this adult prison?* I'd be lying if I didn't tell you that at that moment I felt an overwhelming sense of failure.

God Just Asks for Faithfulness

Fortunately, God has soothed my soul, most days, with the knowledge that He didn't call us to succeed or fail. He asks us to be faithful—

faithful to love the ones that others find hard to love, faithful to love when they don't love you back, and faithful to give when you may not ever see any results. The Bible is full of examples of good men and women who had great successes and great failures (Miriam, David, Solomon, and Peter, to name a few).

Even Paul, the great evangelist and apostle, experienced failure as well as success in ministry. He touched so many people's lives with the good news of God's grace and salvation. But, in his writings, we hear his disappointment with some groups of believers, like the Corinthians and the Galatians, to whom he had personally taught the gospel. Even some of his own associates left him and his ministry work for the world. He tells his son in the faith, Timothy, that *"Demas has deserted me because he loves the things of this life"* (2 Tim. 4:10).

We will always be disappointed if we keep score of our "successes" and our "failures." Instead, we should simply obey God's call out of a heart of love for Jesus. We pour out our lives in faithful service to those the Lord has called us to serve. The results are up to God, not us. God hasn't asked us to do what we cannot do. We can't control the final results, nor will there be a guarantee there will be fruit from our actions. God doesn't ask us to produce fruit. He just asks us to faithfully plant and tend the garden. He's God and we're not. Doesn't that take a load off your shoulders? Our true reward is the joy and inner peace of knowing we faithfully followed the Heart of the Father to touch someone's life.

Reflection and Action

LISTEN

- "Resurrecting Me" by Elevation Worship

STUDY

- Matthew 25:21-23 (NLT), Matthew 5:1-16, Zechariah 7:8-12, Deuteronomy 24:19-21

JOURNAL

1. Have you been instrumental in helping to improve someone's life in some way? How did that make you feel?

2. Have you ever poured a lot of time into helping someone but instead of seeing results you see them take a turn for the worse? Disheartening, isn't it? What can you learn from that situation?

3. Do you see yourself willing to do some things for the Lord, faithfully, for a significant time, even if you aren't seeing immediate results? What might some of those things be?

CHAPTER 21

Friendship with God: The Greatest Reward

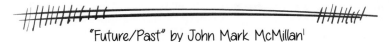

"Future/Past" by John Mark McMillan[1]

The Race Makes Us Better People

I finished the race that God called me to run twenty-five years ago, starting way back in 1992. My time serving the inner-city families in Harrisburg has concluded, but the people will forever remain in my heart. There will be other races. My husband and I have moved to a small college town and I am beginning to see different callings for the next season of my life.

I'm not the person I was before I answered God's call to go "do something" in the inner city. I like the person I have become a whole lot better. I'm not as fearful, as judgmental, or as rigid about the rules. I'm much quicker to extend grace to others.

Before I ministered in the inner city, I used to worry about my family. *Was I a good enough mother? Were my boys serving God like they should?* I felt intense physical pain from various health issues. A few months after I started helping families and had listened to the horrendous stories that some of the single moms had to tell, I had a real paradigm shift. I distinctly remember coming home one day to see my faithful, hardworking husband and my responsible, loving teenage sons. I thought emphatically, *We have NO problems worth talking about! We have the best life. We have so much to give to others!* My problems seemed so inconsequential compared to the tremendous need all around me. I didn't even notice my physical pain as much either.

217

I gained so many things from running and staying in the race to which God called me. It was rewarding to feel like I made a difference in someone's life. Ministering in the inner city made me a better person. *And if you decide to step out of your familiar world and start helping others, you will become a better person, too.*

The Greatest Reward

But the greatest reward I gained by running this race was a deep, heartfelt friendship with my Lord Jesus. I know Him more intimately now. I've had encounters with God that I had never had before stepping out to serve the needy. I've known His direction and heard His voice. I've seen Him confirm His words to me again and again. At times, I had felt such a closeness with God, such a sense of being face-to-face with *My Jesus*, that I became undone—tears of love and appreciation streaming down my face. This is what I call a closer friendship with God.

I would not know God so deeply if I'd brushed off His call and rationalized it away. If I had looked at my weakness and concluded that I was not able to do what He was asking and had ignored His request, then what? So many children and families wouldn't have heard of His love and received tangible help. And I would have remained the same nominal Christian I was many years ago. I was a good person. God loved me and I looked forward to knowing Jesus better, especially seeing Him face to face when I got to Heaven. However, I would have missed living in the fullness of God's kingdom, right now, on earth as in heaven. **I believe kingdom living involves a surrendering of our lives in service to others.**

> I WOULD NOT KNOW GOD SO DEEPLY IF I'D BRUSHED OFF HIS CALL AND RATIONALIZED IT AWAY

Friendship with God is the highest REWARD for answering Jesus' call to serve and love the people that He puts on our hearts. This friendship is established when we lovingly trust God enough to be willing to obey, to go, to get out of our comfort zone, and try to love like Jesus.

I don't know why God chooses to use us to be His hands and feet. I don't know why He lowers Himself to depend on us. Many theologians have offered their opinions. Perhaps, as a Father, He enjoys the relationship of doing things with us. I know how much I enjoy working together with my sons. All I know is that He chooses to work through you and me. Therefore, when we, out of our love for God, willingly do whatever He is asking of us—when we willingly stay when things sometimes get extremely difficult, and when we love people that aren't always the easiest to love—then a special closeness develops and deepens over time.

Having a relationship with God that becomes a true friendship changes your life. It definitely costs something, but it is so worth the cost. It's so worth the times when people misunderstand you, so worth being screamed at by wounded people, so worth the financial insecurity, and so worth the times of sheer physical exhaustion.

After obeying God's call on my heart to go and do something about the pain I was seeing, I now know, in my heart of hearts, and in the depths of my soul, that *My Jesus* and I share a true friendship. Not only is He my friend but I have been a friend to Him. He can trust me. He can count on me to do what He asks. (I hope so. I hope I'll always have the courage to say, "Yes.") To me this prize of friendship that I am experiencing now, and will continue to experience in the future, is a pearl of great price.

Experientially Knowing God

Paul states, "*I press on to reach the end of the race and receive the heavenly prize for which God, through Christ Jesus, is calling us*" (Phil. 3:14). I have talked about answering God's call as if you are entering a race. Here,

Paul sees his calling and life as a race. He speaks of a heavenly reward. One of the great motivations that we can have in our life is that someday we will finish the race of life and go across that heavenly finish line into the arms of our Savior. He will be so happy to see us and tell us, "Well done (put your name here)! Well done!" However, we can have rewards in this life—right now—for doing what Jesus asks of us.

Paul also talks about our life in the present. He describes the joy of coming to a place of having a unique kind of knowledge of God that only comes from experience. In Philippians 3:7-14, Paul implies that "knowing" Christ in an experiential manner—in both His resurrection and His death—was worth more than anything else in this world.

Before answering God's call to go to the inner city, I knew about God. I knew God was love. I knew His goodness and that His promises were true. I memorized a lot of Bible verses such as, *"I will never fail you. I will never abandon you."* And *"If God is for us, who can ever be against us?"* I had read and thought that this verse could be a reliable promise, *"And the same God who takes care of me will supply all your needs."* (See Heb. 13:5b, Rom. 8:31b, and Phil. 4:19a.)

But now, I've come to *know* God in a more intimate and experiential way. I've experienced His presence when I was afraid some evenings in the city. When I felt discouraged, feeling others were against me, or I made stupid mistakes, He didn't give up on me. He loved me unconditionally. I've experienced His provision. I deposited those checks that seemed to appear out of nowhere when we needed financial help the most. I saw how God kept Center for Champions going for many years. Through experiencing Him and seeing Him work, my confidence in God's promises have grown exponentially.

I know that whatever storm I go through, He will be right there holding my hand. I know that even when I'm having a pity party—which, I'll be honest, I still have sometimes—that He's there coming along side me, reminding me of who I am as a child of God. He never judges me in my weakness, but loves me as I am, and gently leads me back to kingdom living. I know I can laugh with God and be silly. I know He surprises me with gifts and special moments that I don't really deserve, just because He wants to.

Isn't such familiar love like that of a good friend? He's proved Himself faithful and I really do experientially know that He is the Best Friend I have in the whole-wide-world. No one can ever take that away from me. No one, nothing, NADA. If that is not a *royal and priceless reward* for answering God's call to serve, then I don't know what is.

Some of God's Friends

God's word has a few things to say about friendship, especially friendship with God. As believers, we are all loved unconditionally by God and He calls us His children. He is so many things in our lives—Provider, Lover and yes, a Friend. But for us to be His true, faithful friend *requires some action on our part.*

Abraham was called the "friend of God" by obeying and believing Him (Jas. 2:23-24). Originally, Moses was reluctant to do what God asked him to do. He had so many excuses. But then he obeyed, and his obedience resulted in friendship with God! We read in Exodus 33:11a, *"the Lord would speak to Moses face to face, as one speaks to a friend."* Do you want to know Jesus face to face, as one who is a friend, in this life? You can! *Trust, obey,* and *do* whatever He asks.

In John 15:13-15, Jesus is talking to His disciples. He is telling them that they are His friends. What did that friendship entail?

> *There is no greater love than to lay down one's life for one's friends.* **You are my friends *if you do* what I command**. *I no longer call you slaves, because a master doesn't confide in his slaves. Now you are my friends, since I have told you everything the Father told me.* (emphasis mine)

Jesus implies that friendship is a two-way street. When we *do* what he asks, He confides in us and shares the secrets of His heart. Pretty cool, I think. What kind of friendship is it if one person is always doing something for the one, but the other doesn't reciprocate? Jesus said to the disciples that doing His commands was being His friend. Consider how great it would be to know that Jesus considers you to be someone He can trust, someone He calls a true friend?

After Jesus was resurrected, Peter decided to go back to his old occupation of fishing. As Peter was out on the water one day, Jesus came to the shoreline and called to him. Peter immediately jumped in the water and swam to the shore. Jesus, Peter, and the other fishermen sat and shared a meal together. Three times Jesus asked His friend Peter if he loved Him. John 21:17 goes like this:

> *A third time he asked him, "Simon son of John, do you love me?" Peter was hurt that Jesus asked the question a third time.*
>
> *He said, "Lord, you know everything. You know I love you." Jesus said, "Then feed my sheep."*

The Greek word for "love" used in this verse is the word "phileo."[2] Phileo means "to befriend" and denotes a cherished love between friends. Jesus was essentially saying that if Peter is saying he loves Him as a special friend, then he must prove this love. He was giving Peter a second chance, but this time his words must be backed up with action. Jesus was asking Peter to prove his love by leaving the familiar life of fishing, and instead, going and telling others about Him. Jesus was calling Peter to use his natural boldness and leadership skills to teach and shepherd those who would become believers.

John, of all the twelve disciples, is considered to be Jesus' closest friend. John wrote the book that bears his name. In the book of John there are several references to *the disciple whom Jesus loved* (John 20:2, John 21:7, 20).

At the last supper, as the disciples were seated around the table together, we are shown a visual depiction of the wonderful closeness shared by John and Jesus. The NKJV is particularly poetic, *"Now there was leaning on Jesus' bosom one of His disciples, who Jesus loved"* (John 13:23). In our culture, imagine brothers who haven't seen each other for a long time, with their arms around each other's shoulders. We can imagine John sitting close to Jesus, observing His actions and listening to every word.

Actions speak louder than words. We don't read that John made bold promises, as Peter did. But when Jesus was on the cross, scripture indicates that John was the only disciple who stood near the cross. It appears that even Jesus' brothers were not there. *"When Jesus therefore saw His mother, and the disciple whom He loved standing by, He said to His mother, 'Woman, behold your son!' Then he said to the disciple, 'Behold your mother!'* ***And from that hour that disciple took her to his own home"*** (John 19:26-27, NKJV; emphasis mine).

These verses always amaze me, in so many ways. We've already considered some implications of this passage but now I'd like to point out the incredible assignment He was giving to John. Jesus knew He could trust John, who truly believed in Him as the Messiah, to love and take care of His beloved, widowed mother, as a loving son would do. There was something special about John that caused Jesus to trust him that way. He was that friend to Jesus *"who sticks closer than a brother"* (Prov. 18:24b). The scripture concludes by saying that *"from that hour"* John took her (Mary) into his home. John already had a mother. We know this because she's the one who asked if her sons could sit on either side of Jesus in His kingdom. But, despite his responsibilities to his own family, John was willing to take on the responsibility to care for Jesus' mother. Caring for her would take resources, finances, time, and was probably inconvenient. But John didn't hesitate to do what his friend, the one he loved more than life itself, had asked him to do.

Jesus encouraged Peter to show his close friendship love by "feeding His sheep." Jesus asked John to take care of His mother. God is looking for a community of believers who desire to be His true friends—friends He can count on. Friends that will consistently love the ones who are hurting. Friends who will go where He asks them to go and stay when He needs them to stay. Friends who will express His love, not just in words but through life-changing, consistent acts of love.

Reflection and Action

LISTEN

- "Future/Past" by John Mark McMillan

STUDY

- John 21:1-25, John 13-15

JOURNAL

1. How well do you know Jesus personally? Have you experienced His acceptance, His protection, or His provision in your life? In what ways?

2. If you feel you're not as close to the Lord as you want to be, are you willing to pursue a deeper relationship with Him? What will help you draw closer to Him?

3. There are some missionaries who exemplify how to have a friendship relationship with God. Heidi Baker and Mother Theresa come to my mind. Do you know others? Consider reading a book written by one of them. I highly recommend reading *Reckless Devotion* by Heidi and Rolland Baker.

CHAPTER 22

Now Go Help Somebody!

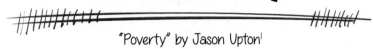

"Poverty" by Jason Upton¹

Making a Difference in the City

I was driving Shante home from the after-school program one evening. She was one of my favorite children at the Center. I know I shouldn't have had favorites, but sometimes I couldn't help it. Her smile, her sweet spirit, her curiosity, and her friendliness all made her special. As we were getting closer to her home, I was reminded that just the week before a shoot-out had taken place on that very street. Bullets were flying and innocent people were in danger. It had happened close to her apartment. The shooting was between two groups of guys, and was possibly drug related or a gang's territorial dispute. No one was quite sure.

I asked how she and her mother felt about the shooting. She responded rather matter-of-factly, "Oh, my mom told me what to do when the shooting starts. She said to crouch down on the streets and hide behind the cars." End of discussion. (One positive thing about childhood innocence is that children are usually not fully aware of the dangers around them.)

After I dropped her off, I could not hold back the tears that had been building up inside, waiting to burst out as soon as I was out of her presence. I didn't want to make her afraid or confused. (Yes, I know, by now it is quite obvious that I cry a lot. But I cry even when I'm overwhelmed with thankfulness and joy.) I sobbed out a prayer, *God please protect Shante and her mom and the others who live on these streets. Please put your guardian angels around them.*

I thought about how I, who raised my family in a nice quiet suburban community in Central Pennsylvania, had *never* had to tell my boys what to do when a shooting starts on *their* street. My heart broke. I wished I could scoop Shante up and take her home with me. But I couldn't protect all 50 children who came to the Center four afternoons a week. I couldn't stop the violence. I couldn't solve the drug problem. I couldn't transform the entire city of Harrisburg.

However, soon my sad thoughts changed to contemplative ones. I was more determined than ever to keep the ministry going, and convinced we did the right thing in starting Center for Champions. There was a real sense of satisfaction, an inner joy, knowing that God was using "little ole' me" to help this girl and her mother. We provided a safe place after school for her, where people hugged her and unconditionally loved her. We taught this fatherless girl that she had a loving Father who would never abandon her. I had seen the joy on her face when she danced on our worship dance team.

Still, reflecting on the enormous problems of the city and whether we were making any difference, my thoughts turned to how appreciative her mother was of our efforts to help her and her daughter. I knew that we were helping this mother and all the other single moms and dads, and even grandparents, who were raising their children or grandchildren. They were so thankful for someone with whom they could share their burdens. Someone who would pray for them and encourage them and offer hope when life got too overwhelming. It meant so much to these people that we were providing a positive experience for their children on a regular basis.

The parents had grown to trust us. We had become a shoulder to cry on, a word of wisdom, and an extra bag of groceries when things were tight. Their parental satisfaction at family dinners, as they watched their children perform or saw their art work displayed was quite evident. At the talks for the parents that followed the dinner, they learned many valuable parenting skills and heard life changing messages from God's Word. The special events CFC provided that pampered and encouraged the moms, reminded them of how much we really cared about them. They started to believe that their lives had value and that God did truly love them.

A sweet sense of peace came over me and I felt God's pleasure, knowing that I had answered God's call to help these ones. I realized that even if we weren't addressing all the problems of our city, what we were doing mattered. We were making a difference, bringing positive change to the lives of several families. So, in a sense, we were changing the city.

Now it's Your Turn

I ran my race. I finished this one, and I know there will be new races to run. How about you? Will you pray and ask God if there is something you could do to help another hurting human being? You don't have to start a ministry. (Although, I really hope more people will, now that you've seen that God was able to use *ordinary* me.) You don't have to *go to Africa,* unless that is burning in your heart. (Please go if it is!) You can make a difference right where you are, or in an area where you choose to go as part of a community of believers. You can make a difference even if, at first, that difference seems insignificant.

Right here in America we have problems of various kinds. There are a large number of hurting people from all walks of life. We hear story after story of brokenness on the news. It can be depressing and overwhelming. There's hateful talk and division—people taking sides, each having some good points and possibly some solutions to offer, but nobody's listening. What good can we do in the face of such need, such indifference, and such turmoil? Plenty! Take heart, and please don't give up before you even try. There is so much we can do—just start with one person, one family, one block, one school, at a time.

I know it isn't always easy to go out and help somebody else. I'll be honest, some days I don't want to be around people. I just want to be "holed up" in my home, in my world and deal with my own life issues. But fortunately, in time, I push past the inertia, comfort, and self-focus and find the motivation to do something to help someone. When I do, I'm so glad that I did and my problems pale in comparison.

We, especially as Americans, can become so engulfed in many good, but distracting things. But our lives and our time are precious gifts from God. As I get older, I'm realizing this more and more. Let's be sure to choose *the best*—choose to put our energy into what matters. I love these lines from Jason Upton's song, "Poverty":

> And where will we turn when our world falls apart
> And all of the treasure we've stored in our barns
> Can't buy the Kingdom of God
> And who will we praise when we've praised all our lives
> Men who build Kingdoms and men who build fame
> But Heaven does not know their names
> And what will we fear when all that remains
> Is God on the throne with a child in His arms
> And love in His eyes and the sound of His heart cry [2]

Let's hear God's heart cry and respond. The world is full of people who need hope and direction, and a feeling of value that comes from knowing that Jesus really loves them. People will believe in God's love by our actions, not just our words. Are you willing to show them? Maybe just volunteer once a week at a youth center, a pregnancy center, or a food distribution site. Or you could host a weekly, or even monthly, dinner for a few teens who are struggling. Help your neighbors. Start somewhere.

Even speaking up for the voiceless, or those who feel or are under attack, is an act of love. **I know for a fact that a person from the**

accepted community can make a difference in someone's life just by intervening and speaking up.

When I was sixteen, my first job was working as a waitress at the one small restaurant in my rural community. The owner was known as a harsh, cigar smoking man, who also drank too much. However, he was always nice to my family and treated me, his employee, with gentleness and respect. A friend of our family, Mary, a black woman, was the cook at this restaurant. Every day, I'd hear this man call her one derogatory name after another using racial slurs and extreme profanity.

One day, I could take it no longer. With much fear and trepidation, I approached the owner and asked if we could talk privately. I told him that he had treated me very well, but that the way he was treating Mary was awful. I reminded him that she had feelings, too. She deserved to be treated better. (I also pressed the point that she was more valuable to his restaurant than I was, because I'd be going off to college soon.)

Surprisingly this tough guy listened to me and did not respond negatively. He changed the way he talked to her from then on. Mary continued working there for many years. In fact, she and his son even went into business together. Mary told my mother how much my intervening on her behalf had meant to her. What did that five-minute talk cost me? Very little, just a few jitters. Yet, for this minority woman who was constantly maligned and under attack, it changed a negative situation in her life.

So, remember you can speak up for the oppressed, even when going about your day, even with your children in tow. Your children might learn something. We have the power to bring positive change to people's lives by simple acts of bold kindness.

The Father has impressed on many of our hearts His desire for His people to *love like Jesus*. Jesus spoke up. He healed and restored lives. I'm aware that loving like Jesus is not always easy. Yet, I know from experience that He will help us if we ask and are willing to take that one step forward. We don't have to look like heroes or address every problem in the world.

I started this book by telling you that when I saw the 1992 L.A. riots, I prayed, *God please, somebody has to do something.* And how He emphatically said to me, "YOU do something!" But how much more impact will the world feel if we would all answer His call. He is saying to all of His children, "Please, DO SOMETHING!"

In the last twenty years, I've had the chance to hear many godly speakers. I have noticed that there are far more teachings on just BEING in God's Presence than on DOING. The message on "being", as opposed to "doing," was first brought to the forefront to counter the Christian "works" mentality, which needed to be addressed in the 1990s. But now it's time to revisit this topic of "doing."

As Christians, we spend a lot of time hearing, teaching, receiving, praying, and singing—even singing songs about the needs of hurting people. All good things. Now is the time to add to that by **doing**: loving others in tangible ways as Jesus did, not just with words but with His life.

Heidi Baker writes,

> So in our quest to follow Jesus, let's not be so busy that we have no time to dwell. But, let's also not spend so much time simply *being* that we forget *doing.* [3]

Jesus said to "go and make disciples" (Matt. 28:19). How did He make disciples? He shared the things He knew about God and modeled them. He healed broken bodies and broken hearts. He spent time with people, building relationships. He had patience, allowing them to grow.

Notice that Jesus didn't say, "Go and change the world." I have known a few precious young lovers of God who have been disillusioned when they couldn't succeed in achieving big, lofty, "change-the-world" goals. In our spiritual revival enthusiasm, some of us older ones told them they could be "world changers". We just forgot to tell them what that looks like:

Changing one person's life—changes the world!

MY JESUS, I LOVE THEE

My Jesus, I love Thee, I know Thou art mine
For Thee all the follies of sin I resign
My gracious Redeemer, my Savior art Thou
If ever I loved Thee, my Jesus, tis now

I love Thee because Thou has first loved me
And purchased my pardon on Calvary's tree
I love Thee for wearing the thorns on Thy brow
If ever I loved Thee, my Jesus, tis now

In mansions of glory and endless delight
I'll ever adore Thee in heaven so bright
I'll sing with the glittering crown on my brow
If ever I loved Thee, my Jesus tis now

William Ralph Featherston, 1864

Endnotes

Chapter 1: You Do Something

1. Matthew West. "Do Something." *Into the Light,* Sparrow Records (2012). CD.
2. Wikipedia contributors. "1992 Los Angeles riots," Wikipedia, The Free Encyclopedia (November, 2017). en.wikipedia.org/wiki/1992_Los_Angeles_riots
3. Confident Kids. www.confidentkids.com
4. Mary Bruce and John Bridgeland. "The Mentoring Effect: Young People's Perspectives on the Outcomes and Availability of Mentoring." Civic Enterprises with Hart Research Associates for MENTOR: The National Mentoring Partnership, Washington, D.C. (2014). www.mentoring.org/images/uploads/Report_TheMentoringEffect.pdf
5. Mary Jo Bane, Brent Coffin, and Richard Higgens. "Taking Faith Seriously." Harvard University Press, Cambridge, Massachusetts and London, England (2005). scholar.harvard.edu/files/cwinship/files/reynolds.pdf
6. Andrew Kenney. "Teen Challenge's Proven Answer to the Drug Problem, A Review of a Study by Dr. Aaron T. Bicknese." Teen Challenge International, Springfield, Missouri (2014). www.teenchallengeusa.com/wp-content/uploads/2014/05/1999_NW_review.pdf
7. Alice Gugelev and Andrew Stern. "What's Your Endgame?" Stanford Social Innovation Review (Winter 2015), 44. 2uqnr73tzny3sl15p2nqglls.wpengine.netdna-cdn.com/wp-content/uploads/2016/02/Winter_2015_Whats_Your_Endgame.pdf
8. Dr. Randy Clark, Global Awakening Ministries. www.globalawakening.com
9. Heidi Baker, Iris Global Ministries. www.stopfortheone.org

Chapter 2: More Needs to Be Done

1. Cory Asbury. "Reckless Love." *Reckless Love,* Bethel Music/Watershed Music Group/Richmond Park Publishing (BMI), (2017). CD.
2. Ibid.
3. National Coalition Against Domestic Violence. www.ncadv.org/learn-more/statistics
4. www.commonwealthfund.org/publications/blog/2017/oct/combat-opioid-epidemic-
5. Center for Disease Control and Prevention. "Today's Heroin Epidemic." (July 7, 2015). www.cdc.gov/vitalsigns/heroin

Chapter 3: The Fatherless Crisis

1. Will Reagan and United Pursuit Band. "Break Every Chain." *In the Night Season*, United Pursuit Band (2009). CD.
2. National Center for Fathering. "The Extent of Fatherlessness" (2017). www.fathers.com/statistics-and-research/the-extent-of-fatherlessness
3. National Center for Fathering. fathers.com/wp39/wp-content/uploads/2015/05/fatherlessInfographic.png

4. Gregory Acs, Kenneth Braswell, Elaine Sorensen, and Margery Austin Turner. "The Moynihan Report Revisited." The Urban Institute, Washington DC (June 2013) 4. www.urban.org/sites/default/files/publication/23696/412839-The-Moynihan-Report-Revisited. PDF.

5. *Family Structure and Children's Living Arrangements 2012.* Current Population Report. U.S.Census Bureau July 1, 2012. www.fathers.com/statistics-and-research/the-extent-of-fatherlessness

6. Brad Jersak. *Children, Can You Hear Me?: How to Hear and See God.* Illustrated by Ken Save. (Fresh Wind Press, 2003).

Chapter 4: God Can Use the Timid

1. Joel Houston. "Take Heart." *Aftermath,* Hillsong United (2011). CD.

2. Randy Clark. www.globalawakening.com

3. Joyce Meyer. *Do It Afraid: Obeying God in the Face of Fear* (New York: Time Warner Book Group, 2003).

4. Bill Johnson. *Face to Face with God: The Ultimate Quest to Experience His Presence* (Florida: Charisma House, 2007) 25.

Chapter 5: Conquering Fear

1. Amanda Cook and Bethel Music. "You Make Me Brave." *You Make Me Brave: Live at the Civic,* Bethel Music (2014). CD.

2. Franklin D. Roosevelt. Inaugural Address March 4, 1933.

3. Andrew Shearman. "Hell, No!" (sermon given at Life Center Ministries International, can be found under the Teachings and Podcasts tab at generation42.org/resources).

4. Kelsie Plante Boehm. www.kelsieplante.com

Chapter 6: Finances and God's Faithfulness

1. Elevation Worship. "Do it Again." *This is a Cloud,* Elevation Worship (2017). CD.

2. Mark Koenig. "Don't Start Your Nonprofit Grant Writing Until You Read This." Website: *Nonprofit Hub.* nonprofithub.org/grant-writing/when-to-start-nonprofit-grant-writing

3. Jason Upton. "Gideon." *Faith,* Key of David Ministries (2001). CD.

Chapter 7: Do You Know God is Good?

1. Housefires. "Good Good Father." *Housefires II,* The Fuel Music (2014). CD.

2. Bill Johnson. *God is Good, He's Better Than You Think* (Shippensburg, Pa: Destiny Image Publishers, Inc., 2016) 164.

3. Ibid., 66.

4. Oral Roberts. "The Fourth Man" (Tulsa, Okla., Healing Waters, Inc., 1951).http://www.worldcat.org/title/4th-man-and-other-famous-sermons-exactly-as-oral-roberts-preached-them-from-the-revival-platform/oclc/1317397

Chapter 8: Do You Know Who You Are?

1. Jonathan David and Melissa Helser. "No Longer Slaves." *We Will Not Be Shaken (Live)*, Bethel Music (2015). CD.

2. Bill Johnson and Kris Vallotton. *The Supernatural Way of Royalty: Discovering Your Rights and Privileges of Being a Son or Daughter of God* (Shippensburg, PA: Destiny Image Publishers, 2006) 35.

3. www.globalcelebration.com/product-category/teaching

4. Strong's Concordance. biblehub.com/greek/3049.htm

5. F. J. Huegel. *Bone of His Bone-Going Beyond the Imitation of Christ* (Fort Washington, PA: CLC Publications, 1982) 52-53.

6. Ibid., 110.

7. Helser.

8. Ibid.

9. Johnson, 84.

Chapter 9: Are You in Love?

1. Jesus Culture. "You Won't Relent (Live)." *Your Love Never Fails (Live)*, Jesus Culture Music/Kingsway Music (2010). CD.

2. Heidi and Rolland Baker. *There's Always Enough: The Story of Rolland and Heidi Baker's Miraculous Ministry Among the Poor* (Minneapolis, Minnesota: Chosen, a division of Baker Publishing Group, 2001, 2003) 177.

3. *The Passion Translation* by Brian Simmons.

Chapter 10: Do You Expect God to Move?

1. Elevation Worship. "Here as in Heaven." *Here as in Heaven*, Essential Worship (2016). CD.

2. Shawn Bolz. *Translating God, Hearing God's Voice for Yourself and the World Around You* (Glendale, CA, ICreate Productions, 2015) 17.

Chapter 11: Running in Sync with the Team

1. John Mark McMillan. "How He Loves." *Live at the Knight*, Jesus Culture Music (2015). CD.

2. Sean Feucht, et al. *Integrity, Character of the Kingdom* (New Kensington, PA, Whitaker House, 2016) 158.

3. Ibid., 158.

4. Bob Deffinbaugh. "When Division Becomes Multiplication." August 13th, 2004. bible.org/seriespage/24-when-division-becomes-multiplication-acts-153-1610

5. Lesley-Anne Leighton. *Holy Given International School of Missions*. www.holygiven.org

6. Reinhard Hirtler. *The Power to Forgive, How to Overcome Unforgiveness and Bitterness* (Shippensburg, PA, Destiny Image Publications, 2009) 47.

7. Heidi and Rolland Baker. *Reckless Devotion, 365 Days Into The Heart of Radical Love* (Minneapolis, Minnesota: Chosen - a division of Baker Publishing Group, 2014) 152.

Chapter 12: Wounded People Wound People

1. Martin Smith. "Song of Solomon." *Jesus Culture Live from New York*, Jesus Culture Music (2014). CD.

2. Barry Adams. "Father's Love Letter." Father Heart Communications, 1999. www.fathersloveletter.com

3. Linda Forster, *Loved to Life*, online course, Covenant of Peace Ministries. www.covofpeace.org

Chapter 13: Wounded Leaders Wound Others

1. Jonathan David Helser. "Abba." *Beautiful Surrender*, Bethel Music/Alletrop Music (2017). CD.

2. Jack Frost (notes taken from a workshop called "From Slavery to Sonship"). See Jack and Trisha Frost. *Spiritual Slavery to Sonship Expanded Edition: Your Destiny Awaits You*, (Shippensburg, PA: Destiny Image Publishers, Inc. 2016).

3. Jack Frost. *Embracing the Father's Heart* (Shippensburg, PA: Destiny Image Publishers, Inc. 2002) 28-29.

4. Ibid., 33.

Chapter 14: The Power of Forgiveness

1. Elevation Worship. "O Come to the Altar." *Here As in Heaven*, Elevation Worship (2016). CD.

2. Elijah House Training for the Ministry of Prayer Counseling. www.elijahhouse.org

3. Raya Jalabi, Oliver Laughland, and Paul Lewis. " 'I forgive you': Charleston church victims' families confront suspect." *The Guardian*, 19 June 2015. www.theguardian.com/world/2015/jun/19/i-forgive-you-charleston-church-victims-families-confront-suspect

Chapter 15: Don't Quit 'Til You're Done

1. Will Reagan and the United Pursuit Band. "To the Very End." *In the Night Season*, United Pursuit (2009). CD.

2. David Hess, Senior Pastor, Christ Community Church of Camp Hill, Pa.

3. AW Tozer, *Wingspread. A B Simpson, a study in Spiritual Altitude* (Wingspread; Reprint edition, 2010) 71.

4. Wendy K. Walters, email to ministry followers. 12/8/17, "Rest is a Strategy" wendykwalters.com

Chapter 16: The Power of Praise in the Midst of Warfare

1. Matt Redman. "Blessed Be Your Name." *Sing Like Never Before: The Essential Collection*, Six Steps Records/Sparrow Records (2012). CD.

2. Redman.

Chapter 17: Joy and Gratitude

1. Sean Feucht. "Celebrate." *Victorious One-Live at Bethel,* Burn 24-7 (2015). CD.
2. Heidi and Rolland Baker. *Reckless Devotion: 365 Days into the Heart of Radical Love* (Minneapolis, Minnesota: Chosen, a division of Baker Publishing Group, 2014) 194.
3. Ibid., 95.
4. Charles Stock. *Glow in the Dark: Living in God's Creative Energy and Supernatural Joy,* (Shippensburg, PA: Destiny Image Publishers, Inc. 2010) 176-177.
5. Steve Backlund. *Possessing Joy: A Secret to Strength and Longevity* (Redding, California: Igniting Hope Ministries, 2012) Day 39.
6. Ibid., 39.
7. Amy Morin. "7 Scientifically Proven Benefits of Gratitude." *Psychology Today* (April 2015). www.psychologytoday.com/blog/what-mentally-strong-people-dont-do/201504/7-scientifically-proven-benefits-gratitude

Chapter 18: The Secret Places

1. Hillsong United. "So Will I (100 Billion X)." *Wonder,* Hillsong United (2017). CD.
2. *Chariots of Fire.* Directed by Hugh Hudson, Twentieth Century Fox, 1981. en.wikiquote.org/wiki/Chariots of Fire
3. Dick Eastman. *The Hour That Changes the World: A Practical Plan for Personal Prayer* (Grand Rapids, MI: Chosen Books, div. of Baker Publishing Group, 2002) 21.

Chapter 19: The Beautiful Body of Christ

1. Twila Paris. "How Beautiful." *Twila Paris-Greatest Hits,* Sparrow Records (2001). CD.
2. Heidi and Rolland Baker, *Reckless Devotion, 365 Days into the Heart of Radical Love.* (Minneapolis, Minnesota: Chosen, a division of Baker Publishing Group, 2014) 152.

Chapter 20: Success, Failure, and Rewards

1. Elevation Worship. "Resurrecting Me." *Hear as in Heaven,* Elevation Worship Publishing (2016). CD.
2. Dave Marcheskie. "Harrisburg Schools aim to improve 'worst' grad rate in Pa." *ABC27 News,* 17 August 2015. abc27.com/2015/08/17/harrisburg-schools-aim-to-improve-worst-grad-rate-in-pa
3. Phillip Connor and Jens Manuel Krogstad. "Key facts about the world's refugees." Pew Research Center, 5 October 2016. www.pewresearch.org/fact-tank/2016/10/05/key-facts-about-the-worlds-refugees
4. Dr. Randy Clark. *The Thrill of Victory/ The Agony of Defeat* (Apostolic Network of Global Awakening, 2014) (booklet), CD or Mp3 available at http://globalawakeningstore.com

Chapter 21: The Greatest Reward— Friendship with God

1. John Mark McMillan. "Future/Past." *Live at the Knight*, Jesus Culture Music (2015). CD.
2. *New Testament Greek Lexicon*. 2018. www.biblestudytools.com/lexicons/greek/nas/phileo.html

Chapter 22: Now Go Help Somebody

1. Jason Upton. "Poverty." *Faith*, Key of David Ministries (2001). CD.
2. Ibid.
3. Heidi and Rolland Baker, *Reckless Devotion, 365 Days into the Heart of Radical Love* (Minneapolis, Minnesota: Chosen, a division of Baker Publishing Group, 2014) 102.

Recommended Resources

INSPIRING BOOKS RELATED TO CHAPTER TOPICS

A Call to Courage: Overcoming Fear and Becoming Strong in Faith (Women on the Frontlines Series) by James and Michal Ann Goll

A Call to the Secret Place by Michael Ann Goll

Answers to Prayer by George Mueller

The Dream Giver by Bruce Wilkinson

Glow in the Dark: Living in God's Creative Energy & Supernatural Joy by Charles Stock

God is Good, He's Better Than You Think by Bill Johnson

Integrity: Character of the Kingdom by Sean Feucht and other authors

Journey to Your Kingdom Destiny: For Those Destined to Live Extraordinary Lives by Rex Burgher

Love Does by Bob Goff

One Thousand Gifts: A Dare to Live Fully Right Where You Are by Ann Voskamp

Possessing Joy, a Secret to Strength and Longevity by Steve Backlund

Reckless Devotion: 365 Days into the Heart of Radical Love by Heidi and Rolland Baker

WALKING BY THE SPIRIT

The Essential Guide to Healing: Equipping All Christians to Pray for the Sick by Bill Johnson and Randy Clark

Living a Supernatural Life: The Secret to Experiencing a Life of Miracles by James Goll

Moving Mountains: How to See the Sick Healed and Captives Set Free by Richie Lewis

When Heaven Invades Earth, a Practical Guide to a Life of Miracles by Bill Johnson

KNOWING YOUR IDENTITY IN CHRIST

Search for Significance: Seeing Your True Worth Through God's Eyes by Robert S. McGee

The Supernatural Ways of Royalty: Discovering Your Rights and Privileges of being a Son or Daughter of God by Kris Vallotton and Bill Johnson

Books and other media by Georgian and Winnie Banov found at www.globalcelebration.com

RESOURCES RELATED TO RELATIONSHIPS

Active Listening 101: How to Turn Down Your Volume to Turn Up Your Communication Skills by Emilia Hardman

Boundaries: When to Say Yes, How to Say No by Henry Cloud and John Townsend

Culture of Honor: Sustaining a Supernatural Environment by Danny Silk

Love and Logic Magic for Lasting Relationships by Jim Fay and Dr. David B. Hawkins

Kendall LIFE Languages Profile (KLLP), a personality profile for individuals and businesses developed by Paul Nedoszytko and Jenni Sanford-Nedoszytko. They provide both tests and counseling. http://paulnedconsulting.com

INNER HEALING RESOURCES

Books and Audio Media

Father's Heart

Experiencing the Father's Embrace by Jack Frost

Our Father's Heartbeat by Rex Burgher, www.klifemin.org

Spiritual Slavery to Sonship Expanded Edition: Your Destiny Awaits You by Jack and Trisha Frost

The Father's Love Letter by Barry Adams, free downloads of *audio or video* at www.fathersloveletter.com

Healing the Orphan Spirit: The Father Wants His Kid Back, audio by Leif Hefland, www.globalmissionawareness.com

Forgiveness

Grace and Forgiveness: Learning to Give the Gift of Forgiveness to Others and Ourselves by John and Carol Arnott

Forgiveness, Gateway to Healing by Linda Forster

The Power to Forgive: How to Overcome Unforgiveness and Bitterness by Reinhard Hirtler

The Wild Love of God: A Journey that Heals Life's Deepest Wounds by Chris Dupre

Counseling Training

Christian Healing Certification Program (online interpersonal and training courses) presented by Global Awakening Ministry, www.globalawakening.com/schools/chcp

Loved to Life course (available online and at Life Center), as well as other courses offered by Linda Forster, Covenant of Peace Ministries, www.covofpeace.org

People Helping People: An 8 Step Journey to Learn How to Help People Create Real Change in Their Lives by Danny Silk, MSW and other courses from Life Academy

Shiloh Place Ministries (Jack Frost and Father's Love materials) books, audio, on-site counseling, schools, www.shilohplace.org

Appendix

Legalities and Forms for Ministry

LEGALITIES:

- If you plan to ask for donations as an organization or ministry you should become incorporated, get assigned an EIN number, and establish yourself with the IRS as a <u>501(c)(3) non-profit organization</u> with tax exempt status. (Google for basic information.)

- Talk to a few local leaders of small established Christian nonprofits in your area. Ask questions about their process and legal assistance in getting their 501(c)(3) status. Set up your by-laws that allow you as the founder and executive director to also be an officer of the board. I have heard sad stories of boards voting out the very person who founded the ministry and taking it completely away from them.

- Ministry liability: it is important to get some type of liability insurance.

CHILDREN and TEEN MINISTRIES

- If you minister to children under the age of 18 without their parents present, it is very important to have staff AND volunteers get <u>Child Abuse Clearances</u>, even if you are not receiving a grant or some entity requiring this. Do it for the safety of your children and protection of your ministry. In addition, be alert and diligent to keep children and teens safe. These clearances do not always catch all the problem people. (Sadly, pedophiles and abusers can actually target ministries to children and teens.)

- <u>Criminal Record Background Checks</u> are important for employees and regular volunteers of your ministry.

- <u>Develop forms for your ministry</u> that require detailed information, such as:

  » Mother's name and address, phone numbers, and medical insurance (if they have it).

  » Father's name and address (often parents have different addresses and last names).

  » Names and cell phone numbers of two other people to contact if you can not reach the parent.

  » Permission to ride in your program vehicles, and to ride in volunteer/mentor's cars (if needed).

  » Permission to use photos of participants in newsletters and social media sites that the ministry uses, such as YouTube, Facebook, etc.

  » Consider asking parents to fill out a Youth Release and Waiver of Liability form for various events.

Contact Denise Wendle

I so appreciate you reading this book! If it has been particularly helpful in some way or impacted you or your ministry, please send an email and tell me about it. I'd love to hear from you. Also, if you really liked the book consider going to Amazon and writing a positive review.

This book is especially suited well for a class or group setting. I invite you to consider recommending it for that purpose. Larger quantities of the book (15 or more) may be purchased at a reduced cost by contacting me directly.

denise.wendle@gmail.com

Facebook Public Page: DeniseWendle.MSW

www.turncompassiontoaction.com

This book is available on
amazon.com